GREENS+GRAINS

GREENS+GRAINS

Recipes for Deliciously Healthful Meals

MOLLY WATSON

PHOTOGRAPHS BY JOSEPH DE LEO

CHRONICLE BOOKS

SAN FRANCISCO

Library of Congress Cataloging-in-Publication Data available.

ISBN 978-1-4521-3159-7

Manufactured in China

Designed by Alice Chau
Photographs by Joseph De Leo
Food styling by Christine Albano
Prop styling by Kira Corbin

10 9 8 7 6 5 4 3 2 1

Chronicle Books LLC
680 Second Street
San Francisco, California 94107
www.chroniclebooks.com

To remember every moment of positive influence, every supportive comment that wormed its way into my brain, and every skill learned or idea garnered that made this book possible is a Herculean task beyond my abilities. A few, however, stand out so obviously that it's easy to name them.

First off, thanks to Sarah Billingsley and everyone else at Chronicle Books. You are a pleasure to work with, plain and simple. Also a big thanks to Doe Coover for having my back.

I'm lucky to have an amazing cadre of fellow writers and food folks to whom I can turn for advice, feedback, and inspiration. To name them all would be absurd. For this book Bruce Cole, Naomi Fiss, Clare Leschin-Hoar, Cheryl Sternman Rule, and Heidi Swanson had specific and notable impact.

On a more personal level, many friends cheered me on with their enthusiasm for this project, put up with conversations oddly centered on chard while I was working on these recipes, and, even better, distracted me with tales of their own greens- and grains-free existences. Jordanna Bailkin, Tara Duggan, Julianne Gilland, Juliet Glass, Frank Marquardt, Kate Ronald, Jess Vacek, and Kate Washington did the heavy lifting on all three fronts for this book.

My family is filled with food enthusiasts. I am grateful to all of them, many of whom have cheerfully tolerated being served the results of my recipe work over the years. My parents, Mary and Steve Watson, have put up with me hijacking family vacation menus for years. A special thanks is owed to Sam Watson and Marianne Condrup for downing many of the results in this tome with good humor, no matter how weird the dinners got (four versions of stuffed cornmeal cakes with a side of stuffed chard and some borscht, anyone?). I'm also indebted to my three sisters-in-law Mary Theodore, Heidi Watson, and Michelle Wolf. Smart, accomplished women who, know it or not, serve as my imaginary audience every time I write a recipe.

My greatest thanks go to the most appreciative yet honest eaters a cook and writer could hope for: Steven and Ernest. You two ate everything in this book, often many times over, with enthusiasm, spot-on feedback, and (almost) no complaints. And that is truly the least of why I am grateful for you both.

CONTENTS

INTRODUCTION

Greens and grains have slowly but steadily taken over my kitchen.

In spring it's tangled masses of pea greens, intense stinging nettles, and tender but bitter dandelion greens. Next, peppery watercress and wild arugula, lemony sorrel, spongy buoyant spinach, and nutty fava leaves show up. Then come pliant grape leaves, piles of brilliantly green Swiss chard with bright white stems, and bunches of fresh leaves with beets or turnips still attached to the stalks. Hearty kales and collard greens (not to mention the usually discarded but deliciously edible leaves of broccoli and kohlrabi) see me through most of the winter.

Where bags and jars of long-grain rice and rolled oats used to stand, the shelves are now full of bulgur and barley, farro and quinoa, buckwheat groats and wild rice. The sheer variety of brown rice—short grain, sweet, medium, jasmine—taking up the cupboard can seem absurd, but I turn to each of them often and for different effects.

Everyone may not be as greens-mad and grains-obsessed as I am, but once you get used to the range of flavors and textures they add to meals, it's tough to turn back. While I'm a fan of most vegetables and all the leafy green things I can think of, this book focuses specifically on greens like spinach and chard and kale that can be cooked. Similarly, I zero in on whole grains that are truly whole, not ground into flour. There are a few exceptions to that rule, but only because a dish was so darn tasty that I couldn't resist (when you whip up the Buckwheat Galettes on page 106, I think you'll agree).

Then, I bring them together. Every recipe contains greens and whole grains. From a light salad of fluffy quinoa and peppery arugula (see page 32) to a cozy braised dinner of chicken, farro, and kale with winter squash (see page 113), these recipes cover every meal and every course except dessert. (See "Greens and Grains for Breakfast" on page 87 if you don't believe me.)

I don't eat a ton of meat, but I'm far from a vegetarian. These recipes reflect that. I use a bit of pancetta here and some broth there; those ingredients are always optional. There are a few seafood meals and a chicken dinner, some ground lamb or turkey. This is all simply how I like to cook. Many of the recipes just happen to be dairy free or vegan or gluten free. None of those are rubrics that I follow or think about much, but if you do, you'll find dishes to cook from these pages.

Not that long ago, it would have been difficult to imagine a book filled with recipes using kale and spelt that wasn't a health book. For some people, I suppose such a thing is still tricky to under-stand. Yet where so many regard hearty greens and whole grains with an eye toward their role in a healthful diet, I see them first and foremost as delicious.

FAVA GREENS

COLLARD GREENS

ARUGULA

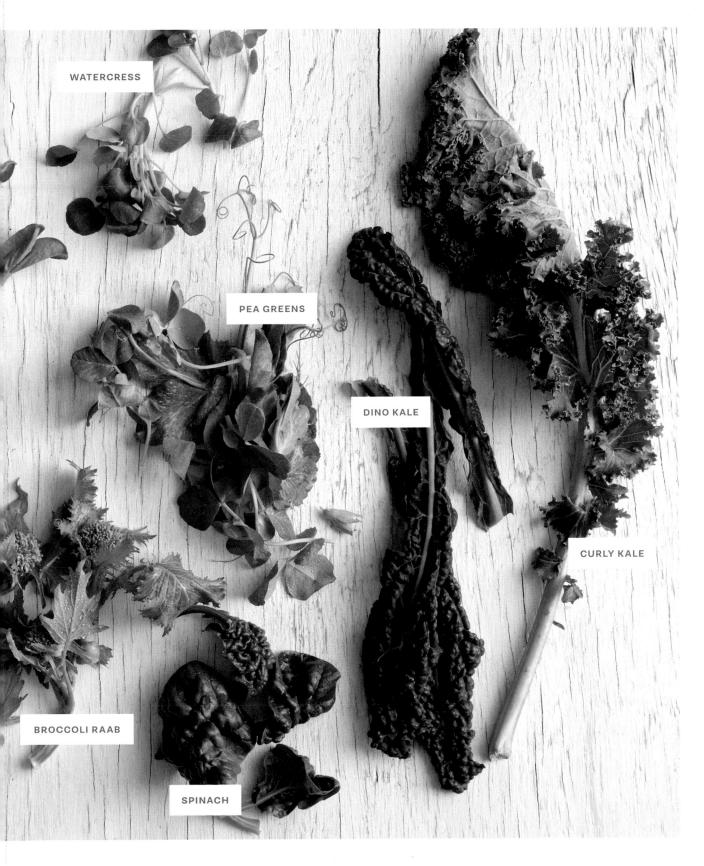

WATERCRESS

PEA GREENS

DINO KALE

CURLY KALE

BROCCOLI RAAB

SPINACH

GREENS

Greens are leaves, plain and simple.

I am no botanist. Nor am I an avid or even successful gardener. When I'm cooking—and eating—I care mostly about how a green tastes and how it can be cooked and am not all that concerned about its family or genus. I consider how strong its bitter edge is, from the bright spiciness of mustard greens to the intense slap of collard greens. I think of the texture, from soft and tender pea greens to stiff and tough kale. Then I account for how cooking either brings out its bitterness (spinach) or tames it (dandelion greens).

Once I've weighed all these factors, I go ahead and use greens inter-changeably, simply adjusting cooking times and seasonings along the way. I encourage you to do the same.

There are more than a dozen greens listed here, organized from delicate to hearty and grouped by those that can substitute for each other. Most grocery stores, however, limit their stock to a half dozen. Fresh herbs, arugula, spinach, chard, kale, and collard greens are fairly easy to find in most locales. Mustard greens, watercress, escarole, and turnip greens may also be regulars, depending on regional prefer-ences. Large supermarket chains are unlikely, though, to carry fava greens, purslane, or fresh grape leaves. For now, such items are still intensely seasonal and need to be sought out at farm stands, natural foods co-ops, and specialty stores.

Luckily, they are, at heart, all green leaves. Every recipe in this book will work using parsley for an herb, spinach for quick-cooking greens, or kale for longer-cooking greens.

SPINACH

Spinach is the gateway green. Widely available and widely cooked, it's the first green most people have eaten in a cooked form instead of tossed in a salad. While I'm all for people eating cooked greens, spinach, so mild and mellow when raw, develops a slightly bitter, even metallic or tannic, edge when cooked. This edge, as creamed spinach aficio-nados can attest, can be dulled with fat, most particularly butter, cream, or cheese.

The baby spinach sold in salad bins or plastic containers should be used as a salad ingredient—trying to cook them is an exercise in frustration since heat melts them down to nothing and you end up with a slippery green puddle from even the biggest pile of leaves. Such tender leaves do work nicely in soups, however, where the heat of the broth can wilt them as it's ladled into the bowl.

Older, bigger leaves and heirloom varieties like the chef's darling Bloomsdale spinach, however, have thick leaves with deep grooves that can stand up to a bit of heat without completely disappearing.

ARUGULA AND WATERCRESS

One of the best developments in supermarket produce departments in my lifetime is the widespread availability of arugula. Watercress at specialty markets is a nice touch, too. Most people toss both in salads, and that is a fine and noble thing, but their peppery flavor works in many cooked dishes, as well. Like spinach, arugula and watercress cook quickly and wilt down into a shadow of their raw selves. I use this to my advantage in soups, where the hot broth cooks them in the serving bowl, and at other times that I want greens to wilt down in a jiffy.

STINGING NETTLES

Nettles prove that a weed is only a weed if you don't want it growing where it is. Stinging nettles tend to be aggressive plants when they find damp locations in the temperate areas where they can thrive. Luckily, they are uniquely flavorful, with a deep green flavor that makes nettles taste like they're good for you, as if spring leapt into each bite. Tame them with a dunk in boiling salted water. While they're still raw, avoid their eponymous sting by wearing long sleeves and gloves, or just put plastic bags

on your hands when you handle them. At farm stands and markets they're often sold in garbage bags to keep everyone sting-free.

Like spinach, nettles cook down to a fraction of their original volume. Since they take up so much room when raw and sting when you touch them, I tend to cook them down right when I bring them home and then store them, cooked, for up to two days before using. Or I pop blanched nettles (see "How to Blanch Greens" on page 14) in a resealable plastic bag, push out as much air from the bag as possible, and freeze them. I then have up to six months to use them.

PEA GREENS

These young shoots and fine tendrils from pea plants are sold in towered tangled masses. They cook down quickly and have a delicate flavor that is easily overshadowed if cooked with too much seasoning. Keep things simple with a bit of oil and small amounts of aromatics like onions, garlic, or ginger to make sure the soft pea-like flavor can shine.

FAVA GREENS

Fava greens have a wonderfully nutty flavor and cook up much like spinach or nettles—quickly. Favas are in the family of "nitrogen fixers," plants that put nitrogen back into the soil, working as natural

fertilizers. Lots of farmers plant fava beans to fix nitrogen in the soil before planting the "real" crop on that plot, with no intention of letting the plants come to maturity or harvesting the fat pods. Some will bring the leaves to markets or sell them to specialty stores. Savvy cooks who have trouble finding them let farmers know they're interested in buying the small, pointed leaves of the plants.

GREEN HERBS

I love using big bushy bunches of herbs as if they were any other green. They pack more distinctive and decidedly less bitter flavors than your average green, but they also toss up and cook down like the tender leaves they are. You'll see parsley, sorrel, cilantro, and mint cast to play the role of "greens" in many of these recipes.

PURSLANE

Part green, part herb, purslane has spongy little leaves that have a wonderful slipperiness hidden in their crunch. Like parsley and cilantro, the tender part of the stem is edible, too. Purslane is tricky to find, even at markets where forage stands (those selling wild mushrooms) are as likely to sell it as farmers, since it grows quite happily in the wild as well as being cultivated. Try it in salads or cooked quickly, like spinach.

ESCAROLE

Often used as a salad green, escarole is a chicory, closely related to Belgian endive and radicchio. It provides crunch when used raw or a hearty texture when cooked, but without the fibrous effect of denser, darker greens. If escarole isn't available, frisée, sometimes sold as curly escarole, or Belgian endive can both be a bit more bitter, but work well in place of escarole in these recipes.

DANDELION GREENS

Yes, dandelion greens are similar to the leaves of the weeds you tackle in your lawn. However, the bunches of greens at markets are a variety grown specifically for their big, flavorful leaves. Those that grow in yards and gardens are, indeed, edible, as long as those areas aren't treated with chemicals. Dandelion greens pack more than the average amount of what many eaters experience as bitterness in every bite. I call on that flavor and try to harness it to good effect, often pairing these greens with acid (lemon, tomatoes, vinegar) and fat (olive oil, butter, eggs) to help tame their wilder edges.

BEET GREENS

I've never seen beet greens for sale all on their own. What I have seen, however, are big vibrant green leaves etched with red still attached to their earthy sweet roots. Beet greens are quite tender and cook up quickly, much like chard (their close relative). Cut the greens off from their beets and store them separately; the roots draw energy down from the leaves and will keep doing so even after they've been pulled from their underground dwelling.

CHARD

The difference between Swiss chard, with its pearly white stems, and its more colorful siblings, red and golden chard, isn't just color. The darker the color of the stem, the more intense the flavor of the plant and the more likely it is to "bleed" and color the rest of the dish.

While certainly edible when raw, I tend to find the earthy flavor of chard, a chenopod like beets and spinach, a bit too tannic when uncooked, an effect that even the briefest connection to heat mitigates significantly.

MUSTARD GREENS

The sharp, peppery, even spicy taste of mustard greens is fun to highlight. Nature packs a lot of flavor into leaves that take a bit more cooking than chard or beet greens, but break down a bit faster than heartier kales and collards. I've been known to use mustard greens in pretty much any application in this book, from raw in salads to stewed in soups. When a recipe specifically calls for mustard greens and you can't find any at the market, dandelion greens or broccoli raab, even though more bitter, usually fit the bill.

BROCCOLI RAAB

I've seen small sprigs of broccoli-like vegetables labeled "broccoli raab" at markets, but what I'm talking about is mainly greens, with a tiny broccoli-looking floret here and there. It has an assertive flavor (that's a nice way of saying it!) that benefits greatly from being cooked with other strong flavors like garlic, anchovies, and chiles. It likes to hang out with tomatoes a lot, too.

GRAPE LEAVES AND FIG LEAVES

Smart farmers are starting to realize there is a market for their excess foliage, and I've seen fresh grape leaves and fig leaves for sale in California. These greens, whether fresh or preserved, are most commonly used to wrap around things. Fresh leaves definitely need to be blanched (see "How to Blanch Greens" on page 14) to soften their stiffness and scratchy surfaces. Once softened, they are easy to roll around grain fillings or plaster around fish before baking or grilling. If you use jarred preserved grape leaves, be sure to rinse them of their powerfully salty brine before cooking with them.

TURNIP GREENS

Turnip greens are, as you might guess, the leafy tops of turnip plants. Certain turnip varieties are grown specifically for their greens, which is where piles of turnip greens at the grocery store come from. If, however, you grow turnips in the garden or happen to find bunches of turnips at the market with their greens still attached, they make good eating too. If you buy a bunch, cut the greens off and store them separately from the turnips; they will each last longer.

BROCCOLI GREENS

The leaves from the broccoli plant are rarely sold on their own, but can sometimes be found still attached to crowns sold with substantial stems. The plants grow tons of leaves, which have a lot in common with kale and collard greens in terms of texture and flavor. They're a real bonus for gardeners cultivating broccoli plants; use them in recipes calling for other hearty cooking greens.

KOHLRABI GREENS

Again, you need to be deeply into greens—either growing them yourself or getting them from a farmer—to have access to kohlrabi greens. The leafy tops of this alien-looking root vegetable are just as edible as turnip greens and beet greens. Like broccoli greens, they have a sturdy texture and assertive flavor that's similar to kale.

KALE

The darling of healthful diets, kale comes in many varieties, from the wide curly green leaves labeled "curly kale," "green kale," or simply "kale" to the trim, deeply grooved but relatively flat dark blue-green leaves of dino kale, also known as lacinato kale, Tuscan kale, cavolo nero, or black kale. Red-tinged Russian kale is increasingly common as well. What all these varieties share is a high-fiber toughness of character and sharpness of flavor. I succeed at cooking kale when I embrace these qualities, rather than fight them. I turn to kale when I want a green to stand up and maintain its shape and texture, even as I try to break it down with rough treatment and high heat.

COLLARD GREENS

Like kale, collard greens are part of the cabbage family. They have the same rough texture, nutritional profile, and deep flavor of their more popular cousin. Both have remarkably sturdy leaves that hold up to harsh treatment, long cooking, and cold weather. Commonly thought of as a winter green, collard greens tend to have two growing seasons, one that starts in spring and early summer and another in the fall.

A FEW HANDY TECHNIQUES

Since greens have different textures, they respond differently to storage. The softer and more tender the leaves, the better they will keep if rinsed in plenty of cool water, spun dry, laid in a single layer on paper towels, rolled up, and kept in a plastic bag in the fridge. The paper towels absorb excess moisture, keeping the greens hydrated but not wet. Arugula, spinach, and herbs will keep easily twice as long—up to a week or more—when stored this way.

Hearty, stiff leaves like kale and collard greens can also be cleaned and stored that way. However, they do just fine simply wrapped in plastic for up to a few days.

HOW TO DEAL WITH THICK STEMS

Kale, collard greens, chard, and mustard greens present the same problem to the cook: They all have the sticky wicket of thick stems that are tougher and take longer to cook than the leaves they run up into. Chard leaves, in particular, cook quite a bit more quickly than their brightly hued stems.

So what to do?

The classic solution is to stew or braise these greens until the thick stem is tender.

Another approach is to cut out the stem from the leaf. I do this one of two ways: I use a sharp paring knife to cut the stem out, tracing its shape within the leaf, or I fold the leaf in half lengthwise so the stem sticks out and I can slice it off in one fell swoop.

With a pile of leaves and a pile of stems before you, now what? Cook them separately, of course. Either start cooking the stems first, adding the leaves later so they're all done at the same time; or use the leaves in one dish and the stems in another. Stems from hearty greens are delicious chopped up and added to soups, much like onions or celery. I even like to serve them as a dish all on their own. Sauté them in plenty of butter or oil and serve with a few gratings of Parmesan cheese and a squirt of lemon juice.

HOW TO BLANCH GREENS

Blanching is the quick dunking of vegetables into a pot of vigorously boiling salted water. Greens, in particular, need to be cooled off as quickly as possible, either by transferring to a big bowl of ice water or running under cold water. This stops the cooking and sets their green color.

Once cool, you want to get as much water out of the leaves as possible. I find squeezing the leaves with my hands works best.

There are several reasons I blanch greens for use in a recipe. First, it softens tough leaves so they can be bent and folded just so. Second, it lets me get the water out of the greens, which is handy when using greens as a stuffing. Third, blanching is a great way to mitigate the harsher bitter edge of greens that some people don't like. Feel free to blanch kale and collard greens before using them in any of these recipes to soften their flavors. You may lose some vitamins along the way, but if it helps you eat more greens, that's fine. As your palate adjusts to the bolder flavors of hearty greens you may stop blanching them, except when needed to make them pliable or to cook them down before using them in a dish.

EATING RAW GREENS

Even the toughest, least yielding of greens (kale and collard greens, I'm looking at you) are, in the end, edible raw. And not just in times of famine or when you're lost in the wild without matches. I rather like the pushback you get when you chew these greens, although I do tend to slice them ribbon-thin to make mastication less of a drag.

Another technique is to break the greens down physically by massaging them with your hands. The motion is much like kneading dough, although I prefer to call it "massaging," because it sounds a bit lewd and raw greens can use some sexing up. No matter what you call it, simply rub the leaves to soften them. And by "rub" I don't mean a gentle stroking, I'm talking serious deep-tissue sports massage here. There's no need to be shy; these leaves can stand up to rough, Reiki-like treatment. The process can be sped up if you use a bit of oil and salt, as well. A salt scrub and an oil rubdown—it's a spa treatment that relaxes the stiffest, most uptight of greens.

MY FAVORITE WAY TO COOK GREENS

I do have a favorite way, absolutely. First, I rinse them, trim the ends off the stems, and then cut out the thick stem up into the leaf. Sometimes I use the stems for something else, but usually I chop them up and set them aside while I tackle the leaves. Sometimes I'll leave the leaves in big pieces, but generally I cut them into ribbon-like shreds.

I heat a big pot over high heat, add olive oil or butter or even bacon fat if I have it in the fridge, and sauté a clove or two of extremely thinly sliced garlic. I often add ½ tsp of red chile flakes or a fresh sliced chile at this point—we like it spicy at my house. When the garlic is just starting to turn color and get a teensy bit golden, I add the stems, if I'm using them. I then add about ½ tsp of fine sea salt and 2 to 3 tbsp of water, cover, reduce the heat to low, and let them cook until softened, usually 5 to 10 minutes. Then I turn the heat back up, add the greens, which are still a bit wet from being rinsed off earlier, and stir frequently to bring the ones on the bottom that have wilted up to the top of the pot and get others on the bottom.

For heartier greens like kale and collard greens, I'll cover the pot and reduce the heat again to let them get tender; I might even add some more liquid to keep things steamy. For spinach or chard or even mustard greens, I'll just cook and stir until they're beaten down, darkened a bit, and the liquid in the pot has mostly evaporated. Adjust the seasoning and maybe spritz with a bit of lemon juice. Eat your greens!

From this favorite method, there are plenty of things you can do:
- Add minced anchovies with the garlic.
- Brown bacon or pancetta in the pan at the start.
- Use dry sherry or white wine or broth or cider or beer instead of water.
- Finish off with a drizzle of nut oil or chile oil.
- Put a poached or fried egg on top.

WHEAT BERRIES

WILD RICE

FARRO

QUINOA

BUCKWHEAT GROATS

GRAINS

Grains are seeds. If you're going to get picky, grains are specifically the seeds of plants in the grass family. Here, I approach grains with more of a culinary bent, treating several seeds that are not technically grains as if they are grains because they taste so good and we cook them as if they were. Buckwheat and quinoa, for example, aren't from the grass family. It doesn't make me love them any less.

When cooking with whole grains it's as important to know how grains are processed as it is to identify which grain you're dealing with. So we'll begin with the processing:

Whole berries, sometimes called **groats**, have had their hull, which humans can't digest, removed; otherwise the whole grain with bran and germ remains untouched. The whole groats of wheat (including its cousins like spelt and emmer), rye, barley, and oats can be used interchangeably in recipes.

Pearled or **polished grains** have varying levels of the outer bran layer rubbed off to make the grains take less time to cook. They lose some of their nutrition, of course, but are useful for quicker dishes and have a less chewy texture. Whole wheat berries, for example, can take more than an hour to make tender, whereas even semi-pearled farro (part of the wheat family) is usually done in about 30 minutes.

Grits or **cut grains** are whole berries or groats that have been chopped up. They cook up quicker than whole berries and have a more porridge-like texture when cooked. Cracked wheat, bulgur, polenta, and steel-cut oats are grits.

Flour is grain that has been milled or ground into a powder. The whole berry is ground to make whole-grain flour; the bran and germ are removed first to make refined flour.

There are a few recipes that call for whole-grain flour in this book—how could I resist sharing those quinoa crackers (see page 43)? But for the most part, I contained myself to using whole berries, pearled grains, and cut grains for the full texture, flavor, and, yes, nutrition, they bring.

I tried to keep to grains that are widely available at natural foods stores and specialty groceries, although plenty of grocery stores may carry only brown rice and maybe barley and bulgur.

BARLEY

Most of the barley that Americans ingest takes the form of beer or whiskey, which gives one little sense of its wonderfully light, earthy flavor and its slightly chewy texture. It is a relative of wheat but has a short growing season, making it a popular grain in northerly or mountainous places where the summers are painfully brief. Barley works with greens of all types, but because of its softness you can use it with tender greens or other times when you want a little less chew from a whole-grain berry, as in barley "risotto" (see page 101).

Natural food stores sometimes stock hulled barley, a true whole grain. More often, however, pearled barley is the only option. Pearled barley can be cooked in 25 to 30 minutes, whereas you'll want to allow at least 40 minutes for hulled barley.

BUCKWHEAT

Buckwheat isn't technically a grain. It is a seed, but not from the grass family. It's in the knotweed family that includes rhubarb and sorrel. Like barley, it does well in cold climates. Like quinoa, another pseudo-grain, buckwheat contains all eight amino acids humans require as well as a deep nutty-meets-earthy flavor. It always stuns me how cheeses and sour cream and eggs can soften its strong flavor and bring out its nuttiness. It's the perfect foil, in many ways, for greens, since it can stand up to the strong bitter flavors or highlight the delicate crunch of more tender specimens. You can

buy raw or already toasted (and much more flavorful) buckwheat groats at natural food stores.

One thing to watch out for: Buckwheat turns mushy in the blink of an eye. Different varieties cook at different rates, too, so test it frequently while cooking.

CORN

Corn can do anything. Or, rather, we've taught it to do anything. We've taught it to work as a starch, a sweetener, and a fat replacement. We've powdered it into beauty products; we've even convinced it to be a compostable "plastic" bag. Here, I'm just talking about whole dried kernels of corn that have, in some fashion, been cut up. Polenta and cornmeal are what you'll find in these pages, where their lightly sweet flavor, which is just a bit nutty, highlights the bitter edge of greens.

FARRO

Not everything labeled "farro" is the same, so there is going to be some confusion on this one. It's not even clear that it is its own grain and not simply the berry of a variety of spelt or emmer or other plant in the wheat family. In any case, it's sold as its own thing, and I find its softer texture and nutty flavor a fabulous foil for greens of all kinds, whether used in a salad, in a soup, or cooked as a pilaf.

MILLET

I can only explain my general dislike of millet thusly: It thrives in hot, dry places. I do not. It has a stunningly bland flavor I see no reason to seek out. Also, it is, honestly, a pain to cook because it cooks unevenly. Getting a pot of these small yellow grains to all be tender without some of them turning mushy is well-nigh impossible. It's familiar to most of us as birdseed and maybe it should stay that way.

That said, millet is a nutrition-packed, gluten-free little number that others seem to enjoy. If you want to give it a try, you can do one of two things: Cook it like polenta, into a porridge, and add plenty of butter or cheese or other fat and flavorful elements; or sauté it in a bit of oil until it turns golden. When it starts to brown, pour in 2½ to 3 cups/ 600 to 720 ml water or broth for every 1 cup/200 g of millet, cover, and simmer until tender, 10 to 15 minutes.

OATS

Like barley, oats can thrive where the more popular wheat (I say "popular" because its flour makes such lovely bread) cannot. It can endure cold and rain. So it makes sense that when we think of oats, our minds turn to Scotland and Ireland. There, whole oat berries and steel-cut oats are as common as rolled oats for oatmeal are on American breakfast tables (rolled oats are whole groats that are steamed and then rolled flat before being dried). It's the heartier versions that I use, and they're particularly good with tender and medium greens—spinach, chard, mustard greens—since oats have a rather soft texture and sweet flavor. Whole oat groats or berries cook up just like wheat berries, rye kernels, or hulled barley—the four can be used more or less interchangeably.

QUINOA AND AMARANTH

Quinoa and amaranth are closely related, botanically speaking, to chard and spinach and beets. No wonder they taste so good together. Like buckwheat, quinoa isn't technically a grain. Yet I use plenty of it in this book. It's easy to cook, has fabulous flavor, contains the complete protein profile we need in our diets, and is now widely available. Amaranth, smaller and seedier than quinoa, is tricky to find, so I've left it out here, but it cooks up into a lovely porridge.

Bonus of both plants: Their greens are edible and tasty. If you find them, use them like spinach or chard.

To cook quinoa, rinse it, rubbing it under running water, and drain it well (this removes its bitter coating). Heat a medium saucepan over medium-high heat. Bring 1 cup/240 ml water or broth, 1 cup/170 g quinoa, and ¼ to ½ tsp fine sea salt to a boil, cover, and turn the heat to low. Cook, undisturbed, until the quinoa is tender and the liquid is completely absorbed, about 15 minutes. Take the pan off the heat, leaving the cover on, and let sit for 5 minutes. Uncover and fluff with a fork.

Alas, raw quinoa cannot be toasted to any pleasant culinary effect. You must cook it before you toast it. Then you end up with a fabulously nutty and crunchy item perfect for sprinkling on salads or anything you like (see Toasted Quinoa, page 31).

RICE

So many varieties of rice, so little time. For our purposes, we're talking brown rice, which isn't a variety, but simply any rice hulled and sold with its bran intact instead of polished away to create white rice. Brown rice can be long grain, medium grain, short grain, and sweet. Basmati brown rice is a long-grain variety; brown sushi rice is a short grain. In general, the longer the grain, the fluffier the rice once cooked; the shorter the grain, the stickier. Many markets offer only long-grain brown rice, a variety I like best when cooked as a pilaf.

Black rice, glistening and dark purple once cooked, is also a whole grain. If you find some, use it in a salad (see page 37) or cook it with two parts water to rice.

Bring to a boil, cover, simmer for 20 minutes, take off the heat, and leave covered for 5 minutes. Then just fluff with a fork. Serve with brightly colored vegetables or snowy white tofu to highlight how darn pretty it is.

RYE

Like buckwheat, rye has an assertive flavor that makes it a natural to eat with dark greens. Whole-grain rye flour is fairly easy to come by, but whole rye berries will require a trip online or to a natural foods store. Rye berries take at least an hour to cook when simmered. Feel free to use rye in any recipe calling for whole farro, spelt, or barley. Rye is chewier and stronger flavored than other whole grains, so it will amp up the dish a notch.

SPELT

Spelt is an ancient grain from the wheat family. It has a reddish hue and a chewy tenderness when cooked, as well as a decidedly sweeter flavor than other grains. Use it in place of wheat berries or farro whenever you like. I've been known to turn to it in times of barley deficit as well.

WHEAT

Wheat is a big category. A lot of the whole grains you find when you venture out into the whole-grain world are, more or less, wheat. Farro, usually sold pearled or semi-pearled, is part of the great wheat family, as is spelt and emmer and kamut and einkorn, all ancient varieties of this common grain. Wheat berries are the hulled kernels of wheatgrass. They can be from hard or soft wheat varieties— hard wheat is higher in gluten and protein than soft wheat. Cracked wheat is wheat berries cut up like grits or polenta. Bulgur is wheat berries that have been parboiled, dried, and then cut up. Bulgur is widely available and cooks quickly, which is handy.

WILD RICE

I don't mean to brag, but I know my way around a pot of wild rice. I grew up in Minnesota and I'm sort of a snob about it. When I visit my parents, I haul back bags of the real stuff—the seeds from a wild grass that grows along the lake edges and in streams in northern Minnesota, Wisconsin, and Canada. The vast majority of what can be purchased in the rest of the world is the kind that's cultivated in the Central Valley of California. It's fine. There's nothing wrong with it. To a Minnesotan, though, cultivated wild rice is oddly uniform, confusingly completely black, and a somewhat sad facsimile of the truly wild stuff. In any case, the flavor of wild rice—grassy, nutty, with sometimes a hint of muddy (in a weird and compellingly good way!)—is ideal with the deep, dark flavor of kale.

A FEW HANDY TECHNIQUES

HOW TO BOIL GRAINS

Boiling, in general, has gotten a bad reputation. It's true, boiling food does make it lose some of its nutrients, which leach out into the water and are then tossed down the drain. But boiling grains, especially the tougher ones like rye berries and wheat berries, lets you know they're completely done before you stop cooking them without having to add or boil off water at the end. It also gets some of their starch out, which you may want for a clear-looking soup, for example. This method works particularly well for barley, wheat berries, oat berries, spelt, farro, rye, rice, and wild rice.

Rinse grains with cool water and put them in a pot that is at least four times as big as the volume of grains. Cover the grains with plenty of cool water—by at least 1 in/2.5 cm and more if you like. Add about ½ tsp fine sea salt for every 1 to 1½ cups/240 to 360 ml water and bring to a boil. Lower the heat to maintain a steady simmer (no need to cover unless instructed to do so) and cook until the grains are tender to the bite. Pearled grains are ready in 25 to 40 minutes, whole berries closer to 1 hour. Drain and use grains in salads, add to soups, or toss in casseroles. Or serve them hot with butter and salt.

USING ALL THE GRAINS

When you find yourself with a handful each of medium-grain brown rice, quinoa, barley, and spelt—or whatever combination of whole grains you have bits and pieces of—put them to use in a grain porridge. Rinse them, put them in a pot at least four times as big as their volume, and cover them with plenty of water (for sweet porridge) or broth (for savory porridge). Bring to a boil, then partially cover and simmer, stirring when it occurs to you and adding more liquid as the grains absorb what's in the pot, until all the grains are tender to the bite. They won't all cook at the same rate, and that's fine. The quicker-cooking grains will turn a bit mushy and make it porridge instead of a bowl of cooked grains. Serve a sweet porridge topped with butter and/or cream and brown sugar, honey, maple syrup, or agave nectar. Chopped nuts and dried or fresh fruit are good too. Or serve a savory porridge with bits of leftover shredded chicken, diced pork, or grated baked tofu, as well as minced shallot or green onion or chives, and chile oil or hot sauce, if you like.

CHAPTER ONE

SALADS, SMALL PLATES + SIDES

CORN, CILANTRO, AND FARRO SALAD WITH CHILE DRESSING

SERVES 4 TO 6

The key to this salad is to cut the bell peppers and onion so that they are about the same size as the corn kernels and the farro. It may seem ridiculous, but having everything the same size helps highlight the range of textures and flavors. Spelt or rye kernels are excellent substitutes for the farro. Barley or brown rice work, too. For those who don't like the unique flavor of cilantro, use flat-leaf parsley or baby spinach leaves instead.

1 cup/180 g farro

1½ tsp fine sea salt

5 tbsp/75 ml extra-virgin olive oil

2 tbsp fresh lime juice

2 tsp red wine vinegar

1 garlic clove, minced

1 jalapeño chile, seeded and minced

Kernels from 4 ears of sweet corn

2 red bell peppers, cored, seeded, and diced

1 small red onion, diced

4 handfuls fresh cilantro leaves, chopped

Freshly ground pepper

4 handfuls arugula (optional)

5 oz/140 g cherry tomatoes, halved (optional)

Put the farro and 1 tsp of the salt in a medium saucepan and add enough water to cover the farro by about 1 in/2.5 cm. Bring to a boil, lower the heat to maintain a steady simmer, and cook until the farro is tender to the bite, about 30 minutes.

Meanwhile, make a dressing by whirling the olive oil, lime juice, vinegar, garlic, chile, and remaining ½ tsp salt in a blender until smooth.

Drain the farro and transfer to a large salad bowl. Pour the dressing over the still-warm farro and toss to combine. The still-warm farro will soak up the dressing in a most pleasing way.

Add the corn, bell peppers, onion, and cilantro. Toss to combine. Season with pepper. Adjust the seasoning. Serve on top of the arugula and topped with the tomatoes, if you like.

CHARD, FARRO, AND FENNEL SALAD WITH LEMON AND FETA

SERVES 4 TO 6

At once both light and hearty, this salad has the bright flavors I associate with spring. You can even make it more spring-like by adding chopped fresh dill, mint, and/or chervil if you have them on hand. For all its lightness, the toothy, chewy farro kernels give it a satisfying texture, like you're eating much more than just a salad. Spelt, rye, or barley are other good grain options here, since they are similarly hearty.

1 cup/180 g farro

2 tsp fine sea salt

1 bunch chard

4 tbsp/60 ml extra-virgin olive oil

2 tbsp fresh lemon juice, plus ½ tsp grated lemon zest

1 garlic clove, minced

½ tsp freshly ground pepper

1 small fennel bulb with fronds attached, bulb and fronds chopped and kept separate

6 green onions, finely chopped

4 oz/115 g feta cheese, crumbled

Put the farro and 1 tsp of the salt in a medium pot and add enough water to cover the farro by about 1 in/2.5 cm. Bring to a boil, lower the heat to maintain a steady simmer, and cook until the farro is tender to the bite, about 30 minutes.

Meanwhile, cut out the thick stems from the chard leaves. Trim the stems and finely chop them, then chop the leaves; keep the stems and leaves separate.

Heat 1 tbsp of the olive oil in a large frying pan over medium heat. Add the chard stems and ½ tsp salt. Cook, stirring frequently, until the stems soften, about 3 minutes. Add the leaves and cook, stirring frequently, until wilted and tender, about 3 minutes. Remove from the heat, transfer to a plate, and let cool.

In a large salad bowl, whisk together the remaining 3 tbsp olive oil, the lemon juice, lemon zest, garlic, remaining ½ tsp salt, and pepper.

Drain the farro and add it, still warm, to the salad bowl, and toss to coat. Adjust the seasoning (you want the dressed farro to be able to stand on its own once mixed with the crunchy vegetables and salty feta and not get overpowered by them).

When everything is more or less at room temperature, add the chard, chopped fennel bulb, and green onions to the farro. Toss gently to combine. Adjust the seasoning. Serve with the chopped fennel fronds and feta sprinkled on top.

MINTY SPELT PURSLANE SALAD

SERVES 4 TO 6

Slippery purslane and sweet, nutty spelt come together deliciously with this mint-packed dressing. Purslane isn't all that easy to find and, unlike most of the greens in this book, doesn't have a very exact substitute. Using flat-leaf parsley or chopped spinach in its place will create a different, although equally tempting, salad.

1 cup/180 g spelt	1 garlic clove, chopped
1 tbsp fine sea salt, plus ½ tsp	15 fresh mint leaves
⅓ cup/75 ml extra-virgin olive oil	1 tsp grated lemon zest
3 tbsp Champagne vinegar	Leaves from 3 bunches purslane

Put the spelt and 1 tbsp salt in a medium pot and add enough water to cover the spelt by about 1 in/2.5 cm. Bring to a boil, partially cover, and lower heat to maintain a steady simmer. Cook until the spelt is tender to the bite, about 30 minutes. Drain the spelt and transfer to a large serving or mixing bowl.

Meanwhile, make a dressing by whirling the olive oil, vinegar, garlic, mint, lemon zest, and remaining ½ tsp salt in a blender until the mint is completely puréed and the dressing is smooth. Pour over the still-warm spelt and toss to combine. Let sit until cooled to room temperature, tossing every now and again, about 1 hour.

Add the purslane to the large bowl, toss to combine, and serve. The salad can keep, covered and chilled, overnight. To keep the purslane crisp, don't add it until you're ready to serve.

ESCAROLE SALAD WITH TOASTED QUINOA

SERVES 4 TO 6

Toasted quinoa gets used almost like Bac-O Bits here, adding both crunch and a hit of their nutty, earthy flavor. The sweetness of the tomatoes in the dressing is the perfect foil for the bitter tang of escarole. The dressing keeps nicely in the fridge for up to a week. Just know that the garlic will get a bit stronger over time.

2 fresh or canned peeled, seeded tomatoes

3 tbsp extra-virgin olive oil

1 tbsp red wine vinegar

1 garlic clove, minced

½ tsp fine sea salt

¼ tsp hot or smoked paprika

4 eggs

1 head escarole

6 tbsp/100 g Toasted Quinoa (see Note)

Make a dressing by whirling the tomatoes, olive oil, vinegar, garlic, salt, and paprika in a blender until utterly smooth.

Put the eggs in a medium saucepan and cover generously with water. Bring to a boil. Cover, remove from the heat, and let sit 14 minutes exactly. Drain the eggs and peel under cool water. Halve or quarter and set aside.

Tear the escarole into bite-size pieces, wash, and spin dry. Divide the leaves among four to six salad plates. Add the egg halves or quarters to each salad.

Drizzle each salad with dressing and sprinkle with the toasted quinoa. Tossing the escarole with the tomato dressing tastes even better, but looks messy. The choice is yours. In either case, serve immediately.

NOTE: To toast quinoa, spread cooked quinoa (see page 20) on a large baking sheet in as thin of a layer as possible. Let sit to cool and dry out a bit, at least 1 hour or up to overnight. Now toast it in one of two ways.

Option 1: Preheat the oven to 375°F/190°C, put the cooked quinoa, already on a baking sheet, in the oven. Cook, stirring every 5 minutes or so, until the quinoa is browned and crunchy, about 25 minutes.

Option 2: Melt about 1 tbsp butter in a large frying pan over high heat. Add only as much quinoa as fits in a single layer and cook, stirring frequently, until the quinoa is popping a bit and browns, 10 to 15 minutes. Transfer the toasted quinoa to a platter to cool and repeat with the remaining quinoa.

ARUGULA QUINOA SALAD

SERVES 4 TO 6

This salad of finely chopped arugula, quinoa, and an olive dressing is ultra flexible. Add, remove, or switch out elements at will. In spring, try thinly sliced asparagus, chopped snap peas, and/or leaves of fresh spring herbs like chervil, dill, and mint. Come summer, diced tomatoes, cucumber, and bell peppers are all excellent additions. When fall arrives, chopped grilled eggplant or winter squash add sweetness. In winter, roasted root vegetables or mushrooms add rich flavor. If you're wary of the raw red onion here, know that if you rinse the minced onion with cold water and then pat it dry, you can greatly mitigate its pungency.

1 cup/170 g cooked quinoa	**2 tbsp fresh lemon juice**
½ tsp fine sea salt	**½ tsp freshly ground pepper**
12 green or black olives, pitted	**10 oz/280 g arugula**
1 garlic clove, peeled	**1 small red onion, minced**
3 tbsp extra-virgin olive oil	**Several handfuls chopped seasonal vegetables (optional)**

In a medium saucepan or frying pan over medium-high heat, cook the quinoa, stirring more or less constantly, until toasted, 3 to 5 minutes. Add ¼ tsp of the salt and 1 cup/240 ml water. Bring to a boil, cover, and lower the heat to maintain a steady simmer. Cook, undisturbed, until the quinoa is tender and the liquid is absorbed, about 15 minutes. Remove from the heat and let sit, still covered, for 5 minutes. Fluff with a fork.

Meanwhile, mince together the olives and garlic to form a chunky paste. Put them in a large salad bowl and stir in the olive oil and lemon juice. Add the remaining ¼ tsp salt and the pepper.

Add the quinoa, still warm, to the bowl and toss to coat. Let everything come to room temperature.

Finely chop the arugula and add it to the quinoa along with the red onion and toss to combine. Add any seasonal vegetables you might want to use, toss to combine, and adjust the seasoning. Serve at room temperature. This salad keeps quite well, covered and chilled, up to 2 days.

COLLARD GREENS AND RYE SALAD WITH NUT BUTTER DRESSING

SERVES 4 TO 6

This salad isn't the prettiest thing you'll ever see, but it sure does pack in the flavor. If you have peanut butter on hand but not almond butter, go ahead and make peanut dressing instead. Cashew butter or walnut butter also works tasty magic. Similarly, spelt or farro or barley in place of the rye, or kale instead of the collard greens are all dandy combinations.

1 cup/180 g rye berries	2 tbsp agave syrup
1½ tsp fine sea salt	2 tsp soy sauce
10 oz/280 g collard greens	1 garlic clove, minced
4 tbsp/65 g almond butter	2 tsp peeled, grated fresh ginger
3 tbsp rice vinegar	1 tsp red chile flakes

Put the rye and 1 tsp of the salt in a medium saucepan and cover generously with water. Bring to a boil, lower the heat to maintain a steady simmer, and cook, stirring now and again if you like, until the rye is tender to the bite, about 40 minutes.

Meanwhile, cut out and discard the thick stems from the collard greens. Slice the leaves into thin ribbons. Use your hands to massage them, kneading them like bread dough or just squishing handfuls until they soften and turn a darker shade of green. Put the greens in a large salad bowl.

Make a dressing by whirling the almond butter, vinegar, agave syrup, soy sauce, garlic, ginger, chile flakes, and remaining ½ tsp salt in a blender until smooth. Add 1 to 2 tbsp water, if needed, to thin the dressing. The dressing is thick; you want it to cling to the collards and rye and not create a puddle of liquid in the bottom of the salad bowl, but you also need to pour it out of the blender without too much struggle.

Drain the rye, shake out any excess water, and pour it over the collard greens. Pour and spread the dressing over the warm rye. Let everything sit for 10 minutes. The heat from the rye will wilt the greens and soften the stiff dressing, making the salad easier to toss. Toss to coat the rye and greens with the dressing. Serve warm or at room temperature, or cover and chill for up to 3 days.

BROWN STICKY RICE SALAD

SERVES 4 TO 6

If you can find sweet brown rice, its sticky texture and soft nutty flavor works particularly well here, but any short-grain brown rice will be tasty in its place. I like the mix of leafy herbs as the greens in this salad, but those who would like more greens should feel free to add a few handfuls of spinach, arugula, or another tender green.

1½ cups/285 g sweet brown rice

2 tbsp sesame or peanut oil

2 tbsp fresh lime juice, plus more as needed

1 tbsp soy sauce, plus more as needed

1 tsp sugar

3 small hot red or green chiles, such as Fresno or serrano, seeded and minced

6 green onions, finely chopped

1½ cups/60 g fresh cilantro leaves, chopped

Leaves from 6 sprigs fresh mint, chopped

12 fresh basil leaves, chopped

Put the rice in a medium bowl and cover with cool water. Let soak for at least 1 hour, or up to overnight. Drain.

In a medium saucepan, bring the rice and 3 cups/720 ml water to a boil. Cover and turn the heat to low. Cook, undisturbed, until the rice is tender, 40 to 45 minutes. If you have a rice cooker, feel free to use that instead.

While the rice cooks, make a dressing by combining the sesame oil, 2 tbsp lime juice, 1 tbsp soy sauce, sugar, and chiles in a small bowl or measuring cup. Set aside.

While the rice is still hot, transfer it to a serving bowl, add the dressing, and toss to coat. Let the dressed rice cool to warm room temperature, about 30 minutes. Add more lime juice or soy sauce, if you like. Toss with the green onions, cilantro, mint, and basil just before serving.

WILD RICE SALAD WITH KALE, PECANS, AND BLUEBERRIES

SERVES 4 TO 6

This salad is shamelessly inspired by one my mom makes for dinner on muggy Minnesota days. She cooks it in the morning before the house gets too hot and puts it in the refrigerator to chill all day, letting the flavors blend until dinnertime. She uses olive oil in her version, but I love the depth of flavor from nut oils—walnut or pecan work particularly well here. If fresh blueberries aren't in season, add a handful or two of dried blueberries or cranberries instead for a touch of something sweet.

1½ cups/250 g wild rice	½ tsp fine sea salt
1 cup/100 g raw pecans	¼ tsp freshly ground pepper
6 large kale leaves	1 red or yellow bell pepper, cored, seeded, and chopped
3 tbsp walnut, pecan, or vegetable oil	4 green onions, finely chopped
1 tbsp brown rice vinegar	1 cup/170 g fresh blueberries
2 tsp brown sugar	

Bring a large pot of salted water to a boil. Add the wild rice and cook until tender to the bite. The amount of time can vary depending on how old the rice is and how it was cured, from 30 to 60 minutes. Drain, rinse with cool water, and set aside to cool.

Meanwhile, preheat the oven to 350°F/180°C. Lay the pecans in a single layer on a rimmed baking sheet and bake them until toasted, about 10 minutes. Watch very carefully—nuts go from toasted to burnt in the blink of an eye. Let the pecans cool and roughly chop them.

Cut out and discard the thick stems from the kale leaves. Chop the leaves. Use your hands to massage the leaves—kneading them like bread dough or just squishing handfuls until they soften and turn a darker shade of green.

In a large mixing bowl or salad bowl, whisk together the walnut oil, vinegar, brown sugar, salt, and pepper. Add the wild rice and toss to coat. Add the kale, bell pepper, and green onions and toss again. At this point the salad can be kept, covered and chilled, for up to 2 days. Add the blueberries and pecans just before serving—toss the salad to combine them or use them on top as more of a garnish for a prettier presentation.

SPICY KALE SALAD WITH POPPED WILD RICE

SERVES 4 TO 6

It's true: You can pop wild rice. It has much less starch than corn, so it doesn't expand as much, but it has a lovely, rather delicate texture and nutty-earthy flavor that works terrifically with raw kale. Any variety of kale or even collard greens will shine here; I just like the dark color of dino kale as a backdrop for the glistening kernels of popped wild rice.

½ tsp vegetable oil

¼ cup/45 g wild rice

1 tbsp red wine or sherry vinegar

1 tbsp agave syrup or honey

1 garlic clove, minced

½ tsp red chile flakes

½ tsp fine sea salt

3 tbsp extra-virgin olive oil

1 bunch dino kale

Heat the vegetable oil in a medium saucepan with a tight-fitting lid over high heat. Add the wild rice, cover, and cook, shaking the pan regularly as if making popcorn, until the wild rice "pops," about 2 minutes. Pour the popped rice onto layers of paper towels and set aside.

In a large salad bowl, whisk together the vinegar, agave syrup, garlic, chile flakes, and salt. Let sit for at least 10 minutes so the vinegar can coax out the spice from the chile flakes. Whisk in the olive oil. Adjust the seasoning.

Cut out and discard the thick stems from the kale leaves. Slice the leaves into thin ribbons. Use your hands to massage the leaves—kneading them like bread dough or just squishing handfuls until they soften and turn a darker shade of green. The goal here is to soften the kale, making it more pleasant to chew, by physically breaking down some of its tougher fibers.

Add the massaged kale to the bowl and toss to coat. Garnish with the popped wild rice and serve.

WINTER FATTOUSH SALAD

SERVES 4 TO 6

Inspired by the divine balance of crispy lettuce, crunchy cucumbers, and sweet tomatoes in a perfect, summery fattoush salad, this version is meant for colder seasons. Switching to whole-wheat pita and heartier greens means the other ingredients can take on some heft, too. In early winter, fuyu persimmons, or "eating" persimmons, which have a firmer texture when ripe than hachiya persimmons, add a splash of orange and acidity; toward winter's end, small yellow champagne mangoes can be found for a similar, although slightly sweeter, effect.

1 grapefruit, plus ½ tsp grated zest

3 tbsp extra-virgin olive oil

1 small garlic clove, minced

½ tsp fine sea salt

¼ tsp dry ground mustard

8 oz/225 g mixed winter greens, such as small mustard greens, baby kale, and Bloomsdale spinach

1 fennel bulb, thinly sliced crosswise

½ red onion, cut into thin wedges or slivers

2 whole-wheat pitas, quartered and toasted

2 fuyu persimmons or champagne mangoes, peeled, seeded, and cut into bite-size pieces

After zesting, cut off and discard the two ends of the grapefruit—you want to cut off enough peel so that the fruit is exposed at both ends. Set the grapefruit up on one end, so it's steady on the work surface, and use a sharp knife to cut down along the fruit, removing the pith and peel all at once. Repeat all the way around the grapefruit so you have a fully peeled—pith included—grapefruit. Hold the fruit over a bowl and cut out each section, leaving the membrane separating the sections behind. When all the fruit is cut out and in the bowl, squeeze any juice out of the membrane and then discard the membrane, reserving the juice. Set aside.

In a large salad bowl, whisk together 1 tbsp of the collected grapefruit juice, the grapefruit zest, olive oil, garlic, salt, and ground mustard. Adjust the seasoning.

Add the mixed greens, fennel, and red onion to the bowl and toss to coat. Add the toasted pita pieces and toss to combine.

Top the salad with the persimmon and grapefruit sections (reserve any excess grapefruit juice for another use). Serve immediately.

GREENS IN YOGURT WITH CUMIN SEEDS AND TOASTED QUINOA

SERVES 4 TO 6

I was thinking of this as part salad, part side dish, part condiment; then I brought it to a potluck where everyone raved about the delicious dip I'd made. Let's just say that this recipe, inspired by an Indian raita of vegetables dressed with yogurt, is quite flexible—and not just in terms of how you serve it, either. It really works with pretty much any green you can get your hands on.

8 oz/225 g greens, such as spinach, chard, kale, collards, turnip greens, mustard greens, or beet greens, tough stems trimmed

2¼ tsp fine sea salt

1 tsp cumin seeds

¼ tsp freshly ground black pepper

¼ tsp cayenne pepper (optional)

1 cup/240 ml plain whole-milk yogurt

2 handfuls Toasted Quinoa (see Note, page 31)

Bring a large pot of water to a boil. Add the greens and 2 tsp of the salt. Cook until the greens are tender to the bite, about 30 seconds for spinach and up to 5 minutes for kale or collards. Drain and immediately rinse the greens in cold water until cooled off. Use your hands to squeeze out as much water as possible from the greens. Seriously, squeeze them in small handfuls, open them up, grab new handfuls, and squeeze them hard again.

Coarsely chop the greens and set aside.

In a dry (no oil) small frying pan over medium-high heat, toast the cumin seeds until fragrant, about 2 minutes. Let sit a few minutes until cool. Crush in a mortar and pestle; or place them in a small resealable plastic bag and crush them with a rolling pin or heavy pan—no need to pound!

In a medium bowl, stir together the remaining ¼ tsp salt, cumin seeds, black pepper, cayenne (if using), and yogurt. Stir in the greens and sprinkle with the toasted quinoa. Serve chilled or at room temperature.

GRILLED COLLARD GREENS-WRAPPED FETA WITH QUINOA CRACKERS

SERVES 4 TO 8

The collard greens protect slices of cheese from the heat of the grill, but also add their own flavor and texture to the final charred bundle of salty earthiness. I serve them as appetizers while people wait for the main event and have found that they are quite popular at group picnics and barbecues. Kale, turnip greens, or mustard greens—any green hearty enough to stand up to the grill—work in place of the collard greens here. Feta is easy to find, but Halloumi cheese, the Cypriot "grilling cheese," works even better. Both of them hold their shape without melting even as they're heated.

4 large collard green or kale leaves

1 tsp fine sea salt

8 oz/225 g feta or Halloumi cheese, cut into 8 slices

1 tsp grated lemon zest

Freshly ground pepper

Extra-virgin olive oil for drizzling and brushing

Quinoa Crackers (facing page) for serving

Bring a large pot of water to a boil. Trim the collard leaves, cutting out the thick stem so you have two halves for each. Add the leaves and salt to the boiling water. Cook until the leaves are tender to the bite, about 2 minutes. Drain and immediately rinse the greens in cold water until cooled off. Use your hands to squeeze as much water as possible from the greens.

Working with one leaf half at a time, spread it on a work surface. Put a slice of cheese in the center, sprinkle with the lemon zest and pepper, and drizzle with olive oil. Wrap the leaf around the cheese. Repeat with the remaining leaves and cheese.

Brush the grill grate with olive oil and heat the grill to medium; you should be able to hold your hand about 1 in/2.5 cm over the cooking grate for 3 to 4 seconds. Set the wrapped cheese on the grill and cook for 4 to 5 minutes; turn and cook for 4 to 5 minutes on the other side. Serve immediately with quinoa crackers.

QUINOA CRACKERS

½ cup/85 g quinoa

1 cup/240 ml water

1½ tsp fine sea salt

½ cup/60 g whole-wheat pastry flour

½ cup/75 g coarse cornmeal

¼ tsp cayenne pepper

¼ tsp freshly ground black pepper

¼ cup/60 ml extra-virgin olive oil

Put the quinoa in a fine-mesh strainer and rinse several times with cold water. Put the rinsed quinoa in a medium saucepan along with ¾ cup/180 ml of the water and 1 tsp of the salt. Bring to a boil, cover, and lower the heat to maintain a gentle simmer. Cook until the quinoa is tender and the water is absorbed, about 15 minutes.

Take the quinoa off the heat, uncover, and fluff with a fork. Set aside to cool.

Combine the flour, cornmeal, cayenne, black pepper, and remaining ½ tsp salt in a medium bowl. Add the olive oil and use your hands to work it into a sandy mixture. Add the remaining ¼ cup/60 ml water and stir until a wet dough forms. Stir in the quinoa until thoroughly combined. The dough should come into a ball. Let the dough sit for about 10 minutes.

Preheat the oven to 325°F/165°C. Roll out half of the dough between two sheets of parchment paper as thinly as possible. Lift off the top sheet of parchment, and transfer the bottom sheet of parchment with the dough on it to a baking sheet. Use a pizza cutter or sharp knife to score the dough into whatever cracker shapes you like. Repeat with the remaining dough. Use two baking sheets or work in batches.

Bake the crackers until golden and crispy, about 30 minutes, rotating the baking sheets halfway through baking. Remove from the oven and let cool completely before breaking the crackers apart along the scored lines. The crackers will keep, stored in an airtight container, for up to 3 days.

MIXED GRAIN–STUFFED LEAVES

SERVES 6 TO 8

By cooking the grains and then filling the grape leaves, you avoid the soggy—even mushy—texture one finds in most stuffed grape leaves. It may not be in any way traditional, but I'm looking toward the end result here. The amount of black pepper may seem extreme but adds great flavor.

2 tbsp extra-virgin olive oil, plus more for drizzling

1 yellow onion, finely chopped

1 tsp fine sea salt

2 garlic cloves, minced

½ cup/95 g short-grain brown rice

1 cup/180 g farro

¼ cup/45 g pearled barley

½ cup/50 g pine nuts

½ cup/50 g chopped pistachios

1 tsp freshly ground pepper

¼ cup/10 g minced fresh mint

36 fresh grape leaves, fig leaves, or collard greens, blanched (see page 14)

Lemon wedges for serving

Fresh goat cheese for serving

Heat a sauté pan or medium pot over medium-high heat. Add the 2 tbsp olive oil, swirl to coat the bottom of the pan, and add the onion and salt. Cook, stirring a fair amount, until the onion is tender, about 3 minutes. Add the garlic and cook until fragrant, about 1 minute.

Add the rice, farro, and barley. Stir to coat thoroughly, and add 2½ cups/ 600 ml water. Bring to a boil, cover, turn the heat to low, and cook, undisturbed, for 30 minutes. Remove from the heat—leaving the cover on—and let sit for 15 minutes. Uncover, fluff with a fork, and let sit until just warm. Stir in the pine nuts, pistachios, pepper, and mint. Adjust the seasoning.

Preheat the oven to 350°F/180°C.

Lay a grape leaf on a work surface and put a spoonful of the cooked grains in the center near the stem. Bring the stem end of the leaf up and over the filling, fold in the sides to encase the filling, and then roll it up toward the longer end to create a neat bundle. Repeat with the remaining grape leaves and filling.

Place the stuffed leaves on a lightly oiled, rimmed baking sheet. Cover with aluminum foil and bake until heated through, about 30 minutes. Uncover and drizzle the grape leaves with olive oil. Let sit until warm or cool. Serve with lemon wedges for spritzing and dollops of goat cheese.

TABOULI

SERVES 4 TO 6

Most tabouli you find in the United States puts the emphasis on the grain. Here, I've put it on the greens. I use lots and lots of fresh parsley and mint leaves with a bit of bulgur for texture. You'll notice that I even consider the classic cucumber and tomato optional: When they aren't in season, I go ahead with the parsley-bulgur combination on its own. I leave tradition even further behind sometimes and throw a hot green chile in the dressing to give the salad a bit of a bite. You can make a salad with an even heartier texture by using cracked wheat instead of bulgur; cracked wheat hasn't been steamed and dried and will take longer to cook; follow the package directions.

1 cup/150 g wheat bulgur	½ tsp freshly ground pepper
1 tsp fine sea salt	Leaves from 3 bunches fresh flat-leaf parsley
⅓ cup/75 ml extra-virgin olive oil	25 fresh mint leaves
¼ cup/60 ml fresh lemon juice	
1 garlic clove, chopped	1 small cucumber, seeded and chopped (optional)
1 serrano or other hot chile, seeded and minced (optional)	2 tomatoes, seeded and chopped (optional)

Bring 1½ cups/360 ml water to a boil. Put the bulgur in a medium bowl and sprinkle it with ½ tsp salt. Add the boiling water, cover, and let sit 20 minutes.

Meanwhile, make a dressing by whirling the olive oil, lemon juice, garlic, chile (if using), remaining ½ tsp salt, and pepper in a blender until smooth. Adjust the seasoning.

Clean and chop the parsley and mint.

Ideally, the bulgur has absorbed all of the water; if it hasn't, drain it thoroughly. Pour the dressing over the bulgur and toss to coat. Let the bulgur sit and soak up a bit of the dressing, at least 15 minutes, or cover and chill it overnight.

When you're ready to serve, add the parsley and mint to the bulgur and toss again. Add the cucumber and tomatoes, if you like, and toss to combine. Serve immediately. Once the vegetables have been added, the tabouli doesn't hold up quite as well, because the tomatoes, in particular, tend to turn a bit mushy, but you can cover and chill up to 2 days as leftovers.

CHARD QUINOA TERRINE

SERVES 6 TO 8

Vegetable terrines are a common sight in France, where slices of them are served up as first courses in homes and restaurants. This version adds a hefty dose of quinoa to the proceedings to a great lightening and flavor-enhancing effect. With a salad and some bread or crackers, it makes a lovely light lunch, as well as an elegant first course.

1 cup/170 g quinoa

1 cup/240 ml chicken or vegetable broth

1 tbsp fine sea salt, plus ½ tsp

8 large Swiss chard leaves

2 cups/220 g fresh or frozen shelled sweet peas

4 eggs plus 1 egg white (reserve the yolk for the Rouille)

1 cup/240 ml heavy cream

2 handfuls seasonal fresh herbs, chopped

Rouille (recipe follows)

Preheat the oven to 350°F/180°C. Put the quinoa in a fine-mesh strainer and rinse several times with cold water. Drain thoroughly.

Put the rinsed quinoa in a medium saucepan along with the chicken broth. Bring to a boil, cover, and lower the heat to maintain a gentle simmer. Cook until the quinoa is tender and the liquid is absorbed, about 15 minutes. Take the quinoa off the heat and let sit for 5 minutes. Fluff with a fork and let cool.

Meanwhile, bring a large pot of water to a boil. Add the 1 tbsp salt. Prepare a large bowl of ice water and set it near the stove. Trim off and discard the ends of the chard stems and cut out the stems from the leaves. Keep the stems and leaves separate. Blanch the chard leaves (see page 14) until they wilt, about 30 seconds. Transfer them to the ice water. Once the leaves are fully cooled, use your hands to squeeze out as much water as possible. Finely chop the leaves and set them aside.

Blanch the chard stems until tender, 15 to 20 minutes. Transfer them to the ice water, cool, pat thoroughly dry, and finely chop.

If using fresh peas, blanch them for 1 minute. Drain, transfer to the ice water to cool, drain, and pat dry.

In a large bowl, whisk together the eggs, egg white, and cream. Stir in the chard leaves and stems, peas, herbs, and quinoa. Add the remaining ½ tsp salt.

CONTINUED

Bring some water to a boil. Grease an 8-in/20-cm terrine mold or loaf pan and line the bottom with parchment paper. Spoon in the vegetable-quinoa mixture and cover the top with another piece of parchment paper. Set the pan in a larger baking or roasting pan, pour boiling water into the larger pan so it comes about halfway up the sides of the terrine mold. Bake until a knife inserted in the center of the terrine comes out clean, 65 to 75 minutes.

Let cool for at least 15 minutes. Turn out the terrine, removing the parchment paper. Slice and serve with dollops of rouille, or cover and chill up to overnight before serving.

ROUILLE

Note that the raw garlic flavor will get stronger the longer this sits.

1 egg yolk	**½ tsp fine sea salt**
1 roasted red bell pepper, peeled and minced	**¼ tsp cayenne pepper**
1 garlic clove, crushed or minced	**¾ cup/180 ml extra-virgin olive oil or a mix of olive oil and canola or vegetable oil**
½ tsp Dijon-style mustard	**1 to 2 tsp fresh lemon juice**

Whirl the egg yolk, roasted bell pepper, garlic, mustard, salt, and cayenne in a blender or food processor to thoroughly purée.

With the blender running on a low speed, drip the olive oil in slowly, allowing each addition to incorporate into the egg mixture before adding more. As more oil is incorporated, you can add the oil more quickly.

Stir in 1 tsp lemon juice. Taste and add up to 1 tsp more lemon juice as needed.

Serve immediately, or cover and chill for up to 2 days.

GREENS-STUFFED CORNMEAL CAKES

SERVES 4 TO 6

These little cakes are best when filled with strongly flavored greens. Dandelion greens, mustard greens, or broccoli raab are all good options. Delicious on their own, they really shine with a dollop of fresh salsa. If you happen to have some bacon grease around, don't hesitate to use it to cook these in.

1½ cups/360 ml milk

2 cups/300 g fine yellow cornmeal

1½ tsp fine sea salt

3 oz/85 g grated Jack or mozzarella cheese

1 bunch hearty bitter greens, such as dandelion greens, mustard greens, or broccoli raab

1 tbsp vegetable oil, plus 2 tsp

2 serrano chiles, seeded and minced

2 garlic cloves, minced

8 green olives, pitted and chopped (optional)

Salsa Fresca (recipe follows) for serving (optional)

Heat the milk in a medium saucepan over medium-high heat just until bubbles form along the edges and steam comes off the milk. Whisk in the cornmeal and 1 tsp of the salt. Cook, stirring constantly, until everything comes together into a ball of dough, about 1 minute. Stir in about two-thirds of the Jack cheese. Transfer to a bowl and let sit at least 15 or up to 30 minutes.

Meanwhile, trim off any tough stem ends from the greens, rinse the greens, then chop them into bite-size pieces.

Heat the 1 tbsp vegetable oil in a large frying pan over high heat. Add the greens and remaining ½ tsp salt and cook, stirring frequently, until wilted and tender, about 3 minutes. Add the chiles and garlic and cook, stirring frequently, until the greens are fully cooked and any liquid in the pan has evaporated, about 5 minutes.

Transfer the greens to a medium bowl and stir in the olives (if using) and the remaining cheese. Adjust the seasoning. Rinse the frying pan and set aside.

Divide the dough into eight balls. Working with one ball of dough at a time, use your thumb to make a wide well in the center of the ball and pinch the dough into a small cup. Put one-eighth of the filling in the well, pinch the edges of the dough up and together to cover the filling, and gently pat the ball into a disk about as wide as your palm. Repeat with the remaining dough and filling.

CONTINUED

Reheat the frying pan over medium-high heat and add the remaining oil to coat the bottom of the pan. Place four of the cakes in the pan and cook until browned on both sides and heated through, turning once, 8 to 10 minutes. Repeat with the remaining cakes.

Serve hot with salsa fresca, if you like. The cakes can be stored, covered and chilled, for several days and reheated in a medium oven or in a hot pan.

SALSA FRESCA

4 tomatoes, seeded and chopped

½ small red onion, chopped

2 hot green chiles, such as jalapeño or serrano, seeded and minced

1 handful fresh cilantro leaves, chopped (optional)

1 tbsp fresh lime juice or red wine vinegar

Fine sea salt

In a medium bowl, combine the tomatoes, onion, chiles, cilantro (if using), and lime juice. Stir to coat and combine everything. Season with salt. Serve immediately, or cover and chill for up to 3 days.

BROWN RICE–MUSTARD GREENS ONIGIRI

**SERVES 4 TO 6
(MAKES 12 ONIGIRI)**

Onigiri are rice balls—a common item in Japanese bento boxes (that's a brown paper–lunch bag to me). I often embrace the concept to use up leftovers (chicken, pork, roasted veggies) and give them new life in a ball of rice. Here, the greens are prepared specifically to meld with the rice, and are cooked until fairly dried out, with flavorful browned edges and a slightly chewy texture.

2 cups/380 g short-grain or sushi brown rice

3½ cups/840 ml water

1 tsp fine sea salt

2 tsp vegetable oil

1 tbsp mustard seeds

10 oz/280 g mustard greens, thick stems removed and leaves finely chopped

Put the rice and water in a medium saucepan or rice cooker. Let soak for at least 1 hour, or up to overnight. Add ¾ tsp of the salt. If cooking on the stove top, bring to a boil, cover, turn the heat to low, and cook, undisturbed, for 30 minutes. Remove from the heat—leaving the cover on—and let sit for 15 minutes. If cooking in a rice cooker, cook according to the manufacturer's directions. Uncover and fluff with a fork.

Meanwhile, in a large heavy frying pan (at least 10 in/25 cm across, but 12 in/30.5 cm is even better; cast iron is ideal) with a tight-fitting lid, heat the vegetable oil over medium-high heat. Add the mustard seeds and cover immediately. Let the seeds pop, 30 seconds to 1 minute. Add the mustard greens and sprinkle with the remaining ¼ tsp salt. Cook, stirring, until the greens are completely cooked, almost dried out, and some are starting to brown and toast, 5 to 8 minutes.

Stir the greens into the cooked rice.

While the rice is still warm, use damp hands to press handfuls of the rice into balls. You want to end up with twelve onigiri, but they needn't be absolutely identical; eyeball it and work with about one-twelfth of the rice at a time. Wet your hands just before you form each ball to keep the rice from sticking to your hands.

Let the onigiri cool before taking a bite if you want them to keep their shape while you eat them. These keep very well, covered and chilled, for up to 2 days. Let come to room temperature before eating for the best texture—chilled rice can be a bit hard.

CRUSTY BROWN RICE WITH GREENS

SERVES 4 TO 8

Most people would serve this take on a crusty Persian rice dish as a side dish, even with the addition of hearty greens and the use of substantial brown rice. I've been known to present it as dinner on a weeknight. A salad of sliced tomatoes or bell peppers alongside adds color and crunch. A slice or two of feta cheese is tasty, too.

2 cups/380 g brown long-grain or basmati rice

1 tbsp fine sea salt, plus ½ tsp

3 tbsp butter

1 yellow onion, finely chopped

10 oz/280 g mustard greens, spinach, nettles, or dandelion greens, trimmed and chopped

1 egg

2 tbsp plain whole-milk yogurt

6 sprigs fresh dill, chopped

6 sprigs fresh parsley, chopped

Handful chopped green onions or fresh chives for garnish

Bring 6 cups/1.4 L water to a boil in a large saucepan. Add the rice and 1 tbsp salt. Lower the heat to maintain a steady simmer and cook until the rice is just tender to the bite, with a slight hint of al dente at the center, about 20 minutes. Drain thoroughly, rinse with warm water, and set aside.

Meanwhile, in another pot, melt 1 tbsp of the butter over medium-high heat. Add the onion and ½ tsp salt and cook, stirring now and again, until the edges of the onion start to brown, 10 to 15 minutes. Add the greens and cook, stirring frequently, until the greens are wilted and tender, 5 to 10 minutes, depending on the type of green. Transfer the onion-greens mixture to a large bowl—don't clean the pot yet!

In a small bowl, beat the egg. Beat in the yogurt and then stir in about one-fourth of the cooked rice.

Add the remaining rice to the greens mixture and stir well to combine. Add the dill and parsley and stir again.

Melt the remaining 2 tbsp butter in the pot over medium-high heat. Once the butter is melted and has stopped foaming, spread the rice-egg mixture in a thin layer on the bottom—it should sizzle immediately. Mound the rice and greens on top.

Cover the pot with a kitchen towel and a lid, and turn the heat to medium-low. Cook, undisturbed, until a crust has formed and the rice is tender, about 30 minutes.

Scoop the rice onto a serving platter, leaving the crust in the pot. Check the crust; if it's not truly brown and crisp, return it to medium-high heat and let cook until it is.

Lower the bottom of the pot into cold water—this will help the crust release. Use a spatula to lift pieces of the crust out of the pot and arrange them, deep brown–side up, on top of the other cooked rice. Garnish with the green onions to serve.

BUTTERY SPICED PILAF WITH BITTER GREENS

SERVES 4 TO 6

There was a small spice jar filled with pine nuts in the kitchen cupboard at our family cabin when I was a kid. Sometimes, when everyone else was outside, I'd take it down and eat one. It was a small jar, so they seemed extremely precious and I dared not take more. Now, of course, the price of pine nuts is sky-high. Yet the rest of this dish is so humble and modest that I feel the price of 3 tbsp of pine nuts is worth it for the sweet flavor and soft texture they add to the mix. But if you feel differently, leave them out or add chopped nuts of your choice. If you don't feel like making the spiced butter to drip over the dish at the end, know that the pilaf is completely edible (some may even say delicious) without it. My favorite version of this uses half cracked wheat and half quinoa. Tip: When you rinse the greens, don't spin them dry; leave water clinging to them, which will help them wilt quickly in the pan.

1 cup/225 g green or black lentils	1 tsp ground cumin
4 tbsp/55 g butter	2 tsp ground coriander
1 yellow onion, halved and cut into thin slices	1 tbsp tomato paste
½ tsp fine sea salt	1 cup/150 g cracked wheat or 1 cup/170 g quinoa
8 oz/225 g dandelion greens or mustard greens	1½ cups/360 ml chicken or vegetable broth
2 garlic cloves, minced	½ tsp red chile flakes or 1 tsp ancho chile powder
3 tbsp pine nuts (optional)	

Bring some water to a boil. Rinse the lentils and pick them over, removing any debris. Put them in a medium bowl and cover with the boiling water. Let sit while you prep the other ingredients.

Melt 2 tbsp of the butter in a sauté pan or pot over medium-high heat. Add the onion and salt and cook, stirring often, until the onion browns, about 10 minutes.

While the onion browns, trim off and discard any tough ends of the greens. Chop the greens, put in a colander, and rinse.

Add the garlic and pine nuts (if using) to the onion, and cook, stirring frequently, until the garlic turns golden, 2 to 3 minutes. Add the cumin and coriander and cook until the spices sizzle, about 30 seconds. Add the tomato paste, stirring to combine everything. Add the greens, including any water clinging to the leaves from being rinsed, stir to combine, and cook, stirring frequently, until wilted and tender, about 3 minutes. Add the cracked wheat and stir to combine.

Drain the lentils and add them to the pan along with the chicken broth. Bring to a boil, cover, and turn the heat to low. Cook, undisturbed, for 15 minutes. Remove from the heat and let sit, covered, for 5 minutes.

Just before the pilaf is done, melt the remaining 2 tbsp butter in a small frying pan. Add the chile flakes and let sizzle for about 30 seconds. Pour the spiced butter over the pilaf just before serving. Like most rice dishes, this one is best served warm, but it can stand up to being covered with foil and kept warm for a while as the rest of the meal finishes cooking; it isn't a disaster if eaten at more of a lukewarm temperature as part of a buffet.

GREEN WHOLE-WHEAT FLATBREAD

SERVES 4 TO 8 (MAKES 8 FLATBREADS)

This is a green and spicy take on the Indian flatbread called paratha. A simple dough is folded over itself to create layers and then quickly cooked on a griddle. Pretty much any green works here; you need to make sure you have 1 cup packed after the greens have been blanched and squeezed dry. The result is a shockingly bright-green bread. Perfect, dare I say, for St. Patrick's Day.

6 large collard green leaves

1½ cups/180 g whole-wheat pastry flour, plus more for dusting

¼ cup/10 g fresh cilantro leaves

2 serrano chiles, halved and seeded

½ tsp fine sea salt

6 tbsp warm water

6 tbsp ghee (melted butter with the white foam skimmed off)

Bring a large pot of water to a boil. Dunk in the collard greens for 2 minutes. Drain and immediately rinse in cold water. Use your hands to squeeze out as much water as possible from the greens. Squeeze several small handfuls hard to wring them really dry.

Put the blanched collard greens, flour, cilantro, chiles, and salt in a food processor. Pulse several times to combine, then whirl the mixture for about 30 seconds. With the machine running, add the warm water to form a smooth ball of dough.

Turn the dough out onto a work surface and roll into an 8-in-/20-cm-long snake. Cut into eight pieces. Working with one piece of dough at a time, roll into a 6-in/15-cm circle, brush with ghee, fold in half, brush with ghee, and fold in half again. You should have a rounded triangle. Roll this out, dusting with flour as needed to prevent sticking, to make a triangle with sides about 6 in/15 cm long. Repeat with the remaining dough.

Heat a griddle or heavy-bottomed frying pan (cast iron is ideal) over medium-high heat until the surface is very hot. Brush a flatbread with ghee, set it ghee-side down on the griddle, and cook until crisp with browned spots, about 3 minutes. Brush the top with ghee, flip, and cook until the other side is similarly crisp and browned, about 3 minutes more. Repeat with the remaining flatbreads. Keep the flatbreads warm wrapped in a kitchen towel or foil. Serve hot or warm.

CHAPTER TWO

SOUPS

BASIC GREENS AND GRAINS SOUP

SERVES 4 TO 6

This basic recipe sets the stage for all kinds of experimentation. The combination of barley or farro and chard is a particular favorite at my house, where we almost always add the optional beans and chili powder (see Variations, following). Seriously, any green you can cook works in this recipe, which is more template than formula; just adjust the total cooking time. I like to cook the grains separately so the broth doesn't get starchy, but feel free to cook the grains in the soup—just add an extra 1 to 2 cups/240 to 480 ml water and cook until they're just tender to the bite before adding the greens. If you want to use quinoa or bulgur or another quicker-cooking grain, add it at the end along with the greens.

1 cup/180 g whole grains such as barley, farro, spelt, wheat berries, or any type of brown rice

Fine sea salt

10 oz/280 g greens

3 tbsp extra-virgin olive oil

2 garlic cloves, minced

6 cups/1.4 L chicken or vegetable broth

Freshly ground pepper

Rinse the grains. Put the grains and 2 tsp salt in a medium pot and cover generously with water. Bring to a boil, lower the heat to maintain a steady simmer, and cook until the grains are tender to the bite; the exact amount of time will depend on the grain used, from 15 minutes for quinoa to up to 60 minutes for rye kernels. Drain and set aside.

If using greens with thick stems, like chard or kale, cut the stems out from the leaves. Trim the stems and finely chop them, then cut the leaves into thin ribbons; keep the stems and leaves separate. If using greens without thick stems, simply chop the leaves into ribbons or bite-size pieces.

Heat 1 tbsp of the olive oil in a soup pot over medium-high heat. Add the stems and cook, stirring frequently, until they're soft, about 5 minutes. Add the garlic and stir to combine. Add the chicken broth and cooked grains and bring just to a boil. Add the greens, stir to combine, and cook until wilted and tender, just 1 or 2 minutes for spinach, 5 minutes for chard, and up to 10 minutes for hearty kale.

CONTINUED

Season with salt. Serve warm with a grind or two of pepper. Leftovers will keep, covered and chilled, for 2 or 3 days. This soup also freezes nicely for up to 6 months.

VARIATIONS

- Add 2 cups/430 g or one 14- to 15-oz/400- to 430-g can cooked beans such as white beans, chickpeas, or cranberry beans with the cooked grains.

- Drop a Parmesan cheese rind into the broth while the greens simmer, and garnish with freshly grated Parmesan cheese.

- Use chopped onion, chopped celery, and chopped carrot with or in place of the greens' stems.

- Spice things up with 1 tsp ancho chile powder or ½ tsp red chile flakes with the garlic.

- Squeeze in the juice of 1 lemon at the end and/or a bit of grated lemon zest.

STINGING NETTLE SOUP WITH RYE CRISPS

SERVES 4

Turning stinging nettles into soup is one of the best ways to harness their unique flavor. While truly young and tender, nettles can be handled bare-handed, I never take that risk and always use gloves (and wear long sleeves) when dealing with them—at least until I've tamed them by giving them a solid dunk in boiling water. The grains in this recipe are a separate item—I couldn't resist sharing this recipe for classic Scandinavian all-rye crispbreads. Crumble them into the soup or use them as vehicles for tangy chèvre or another soft, spreadable cheese to round out this meal.

8 oz/225 g stinging nettles

1 tbsp fine sea salt, plus 1 tsp

2 tbsp butter

1 yellow onion, chopped

1 lb/455 g potatoes, peeled and chopped

6 cups/1.4 L chicken or vegetable broth or water

½ tsp freshly ground pepper

¼ tsp freshly grated nutmeg

½ cup/120 ml heavy cream (optional)

Sour cream or plain whole-milk yogurt for garnish (optional)

Rye Crisps (recipe follows) for garnishing (optional)

Bring a large pot of water to a boil. Add the nettles and the 1 tbsp salt. Cook until the nettles are wilted, 1 to 2 minutes. Drain and immediately rinse the nettles in very cold water (this will help "set" their beautiful green color). Use your hands to squeeze out as much water as possible from the nettles. Set aside.

Melt 1 tbsp of the butter in a large pot over medium-high heat. Add the onion and remaining 1 tsp salt. Cook, stirring occasionally, until the onion is soft, about 3 minutes.

Add the potatoes and chicken broth. Bring to a boil, lower the heat to maintain a steady simmer, and cook for 15 minutes. Add the nettles and cook until the potatoes are very tender, about 10 minutes.

Purée the soup with an immersion blender or in a blender or food processor, working in batches as necessary (keep a kitchen towel over the top of the blender to prevent burning, and potentially staining, splatters). For a silken, super-smooth soup with a less fibrous texture, run the purée through a food mill or sieve.

CONTINUED

Stir in the remaining 1 tbsp butter, pepper, nutmeg, and cream (if using). Adjust the seasoning.

Serve hot, garnished with sour cream and rye crisps, if you like. This soup keeps nicely in the fridge for up to 3 days and can be frozen for up to 6 months.

RYE CRISPS

3½ cups/400 g whole-grain dark rye flour, plus more for dusting

1 tsp fine sea salt

2¼ tsp active dry yeast

1½ cups/375 ml warm water (about 95°F/35°C is perfect—nothing over 110°F/43°C)

Combine the flour and salt in a large bowl. Dissolve the yeast in the warm water in a small bowl and let sit until foamy, about 5 minutes. Pour the yeast and water into the flour mixture and stir until combined into a wet, sticky dough. Cover and let sit until the dough is slightly puffy and softer looking, at least 1 hour or up to 4 hours. This dough is flexible—if you let it sit for a while, it will be fine.

Preheat the oven to 375°F/190°C. Prepare one or two baking sheets by covering them with parchment paper. Divide the dough into twelve pieces. Dust the dough and work surface with plenty of flour, and roll out each section of dough until it's almost paper-thin and measures about 8 by 16 in/20 by 40.5 cm. Place each section of dough on a baking sheet and bake until brown at the edges and crisp, 16 to 18 minutes.

Transfer the parchment and crisps to a cooling rack. Repeat with the remaining dough.

The crackers will crisp up as they cool, about 20 minutes. Store in an airtight container for up to 3 days.

CHILLED WATERCRESS YOGURT SOUP WITH WHEAT BERRIES

SERVES 4

I'm a huge fan of cold soups when the weather turns hot. Even those that require some cooking, like this one, can be made in the cool of the morning, allowed to chill all day, and then brought out when everyone is hungry but no one wants to turn on a burner or move a muscle. This soup may sound a bit odd, but the chewy texture of the wheat berries adds some heft to an otherwise svelte and light summer treat. The tang of yogurt is part of this soup's charm, but an equal amount of heavy cream makes an even creamier soup.

1 cup/190 g wheat berries

2 tsp fine sea salt

5 cups/200 g watercress

1 tbsp extra-virgin olive oil, plus more for drizzling

8 green onions, chopped

1 garlic clove, minced

3 cups/720 ml chicken or vegetable broth

1 cup/240 ml plain whole-milk yogurt

Freshly ground black or white pepper

Fresh mint, dill, or chervil for garnish (optional)

Rinse the wheat berries. Put them in a medium saucepan and cover with water. Bring to a boil, add 1 tsp of the salt, lower the heat to maintain a steady simmer, and cook, stirring now and again, until the wheat berries are tender to the bite, 40 to 60 minutes. Drain off any excess water.

Meanwhile, clean the watercress as needed.

Heat the olive oil in a soup pot over medium-high heat. Add the green onions and remaining 1 tsp salt. Cook, stirring frequently, until the onions soften, about 1 minute. Add the garlic and cook, stirring, until softened, about 1 minute more. Add the chicken broth and watercress and bring to a boil. Remove from the heat and let cool slightly.

Purée the soup with an immersion blender or in a blender or food processor, working in batches as necessary (keep a kitchen towel over the top of the blender to prevent burning, and potentially stain-ing, splatters). For a silken, super-smooth soup with a less fibrous texture, run the purée through a food mill or sieve.

Whisk in the yogurt. Stir in the drained wheat berries. Adjust the seasoning. Chill for at least 1 hour, or up to overnight. Serve cold, garnished with fresh mint, if you like, and a drizzle of olive oil.

SPICY GREENS SOUP WITH BULGUR DUMPLINGS

SERVES 4 TO 6

The bulgur dumplings in this soup take their cue from kofte, a mixture of bulgur, onion, and often ground lamb. Whether you use lamb, beef, pork, or turkey to hold the bulgur together, the meat adds hearty texture to this spicy, flavorful soup. I love escarole here since the leaves keep a bit of their crispness, and the bitter edge works particularly well with the spicy tomato broth, but kale or collard greens work nicely, too.

1 cup/150 g wheat bulgur	2 tbsp tomato paste
1 yellow onion	½ tsp red chile flakes
8 oz/225 g ground lamb, beef, pork, or turkey	6 cups/1.4 L chicken or vegetable broth
2 tsp fine sea salt	1 head escarole
4 fresh or canned tomatoes	2 tbsp butter
1 tbsp extra-virgin olive oil	10 fresh mint leaves, minced
2 garlic cloves, thinly sliced	½ tsp freshly ground pepper

Soak the bulgur in water for 5 minutes. While the bulgur soaks, peel and quarter the onion. Chop three of the quarters and set aside. Mince the fourth quarter.

Drain the bulgur and combine with the minced onion, ground lamb, and 1 tsp of the salt in a bowl. Lightly knead the mixture with damp hands to form a workable dough, adding water 1 tsp at a time, as needed, to make the dough soft and smooth. Pull the dough apart into twenty-four even bits and roll them into meatballs, each about 1 in/2.5 cm in diameter. Set the bulgur meatballs on a plate, cover, and chill for at least 30 minutes, or up to overnight.

Meanwhile, bring a medium pot of water to a boil. If using fresh tomatoes, cut a small x in the bottom of each tomato, then drop them in the boiling water, leaving them there until their peels start to pull away at the x, about 30 seconds. Use a slotted spoon to lift them out of the water (leave the pot of boiling water to simmer—you'll need it to cook the meatballs in a second). Run the tomatoes quickly under cold running water to cool them off or simply set them on a cutting board and let them sit for a few minutes. When they're cool enough to handle, use a paring knife to lift off their peels starting where they are coming away. Cut the tomatoes in half crosswise and squeeze out any seeds. Whatever tomatoes you're using, finely chop them and set them aside.

Heat the olive oil in a soup pot over medium-high heat. Add the chopped onion and remaining 1 tsp salt and cook, stirring occasionally, until the onion starts to brown, about 5 minutes. Add the garlic and cook, stirring constantly, until the garlic turns golden, about 1 minute. Add the tomato paste, tomatoes, and chile flakes and cook, stirring, until the tomato paste and onion are well combined. Add the chicken broth and bring to a simmer, and then lower the heat to maintain a simmer.

Meanwhile, trim and chop the escarole into bite-size pieces. Add them to the soup pot and cook, simmering, until the escarole is very tender, about 10 minutes. Adjust the seasoning.

With the simmering pot of water, plop in the meatballs and simmer until tender and cooked through, about 5 minutes. Lift the meatballs out with a slotted spoon and set to drain on a layer of paper towels for a moment before adding them to the soup.

Melt the butter in a small frying pan over medium-high heat. Add the mint and pepper and let them sizzle for a few seconds. Drizzle the flavored butter into the soup. Serve immediately.

ARUGULA SOBA NOODLE SOUP

SERVES 4

Soba noodles are classically made with 100 percent buckwheat flour, and those are the ones I seek out whenever possible. Those made with a mix of buckwheat and whole wheat are more commonly available and are still plenty tasty.

8 cups/2 L chicken or vegetable broth

5 thin slices peeled fresh ginger

2 garlic cloves, peeled

4 whole star anise

2 tbsp tamari or soy sauce, plus more for serving

1 tbsp mirin (optional)

6 handfuls small-leaf arugula

12 oz/340 g soba noodles

12 oz/340 g firm tofu, thinly sliced, or cooked chicken or pork or shrimp, thinly sliced

2 green onions, finely chopped (optional)

Mixed fresh green herb leaves, such as cilantro, basil, or mint, for garnish (optional)

Hot chile oil for serving

Toasted sesame oil for serving

Put the chicken broth, ginger, garlic, and star anise in a soup pot. Bring just to a boil, lower the heat to maintain a steady simmer, and cook, undisturbed, for 20 minutes. Fish out and discard the ginger and star anise. Stir in the tamari and mirin (if using).

Meanwhile, bring a large pot of water to a boil. Divide the arugula among four large soup bowls.

When the water boils, cook the soba noodles according to the package directions. Drain, quickly rinse with cool running water, and divide the soba among the bowls, dropping them on top of the arugula. Top the soba with tofu and ladle enough broth into each bowl to wilt the arugula and cover the noodles. Garnish with the green onion and herbs, if you like.

Serve immediately with tamari, chile oil, and toasted sesame oil at the table, for people to add as they like.

LEEK AND SORREL CHICKEN SOUP WITH STEEL-CUT OATS

SERVES 4

Unless you plant it yourself, sorrel and its bright lemon-like flavor can be tricky to find. One farmer told me there just isn't much demand for it, even from chefs, so they stopped growing it. Luckily, any flavorful tender green—watercress or tiny pepper cress, arugula, or borage—works wonderfully in its place. Even workaday spinach will highlight the fresh, light nature of this cozy soup. While this recipe calls for steel-cut oats, this take on chicken soup is equally yummy when made with the even heartier barley.

1 chicken (about 4 lb/1.8 kg)	**Fine sea salt**
3 qt/2.8 L water	**¾ cup/110 g steel-cut oats**
4 leeks	**4 oz/115 g sorrel or other tender greens, chopped**
10 peppercorns	**Freshly ground pepper**
4 whole cloves	

Put the chicken in a large soup pot and add the water. Bring to a boil.

Meanwhile, trim the leeks. Cut off the dark green parts, rinse them thoroughly, and add them to the pot with the chicken. Add the peppercorns, cloves, and 1 tbsp salt. Cut the white and light green parts of the leek in half lengthwise and finely slice them. Rinse them, if needed, and set aside.

After everything in the pot comes to a boil, lower the heat to maintain a steady simmer and cook until the chicken is cooked through, about 1 hour.

Remove the chicken from the pot and let it sit until cool enough to handle. Remove the dark green leek parts and discard. If you see the peppercorns and/or cloves, fish them out as well and discard.

Add the oats and sliced leeks and bring the broth to a boil. Lower the heat to maintain a steady simmer, and cook until the oats are tender, about 40 minutes.

When the chicken is cool enough to handle, remove and discard the skin. Pull the meat from the bones, shredding it as you go. You should have about 4 cups/500 g of shredded cooked chicken, but this soup is flexible, and anywhere from 3 cups/375 g to 5 cups/625 g is dandy.

When the oats are tender, return the shredded chicken to the pot along with the sorrel. Cook until the sorrel is wilted and tender and the chicken is heated through, 1 to 2 minutes. Season with salt and pepper.

Serve hot. Store soup in the fridge overnight or freeze for up to 6 months.

ALL BLACK KALE, LENTIL, AND QUINOA SOUP

SERVES 6

Lots of dark colors reflect the deep earthy flavor of this soup, which is thick enough to pass as a stew. Add some chopped bacon or pancetta with the onion or drop a ham hock into the pot with the lentils if you want to add a back note of meaty flavor to this already hearty soup. If it's Halloween, add two peeled and chopped carrots along with the celery for a black-and-orange dinner.

4 tbsp/60 ml extra-virgin olive oil	¼ tsp ground cinnamon
1 yellow onion, finely chopped	¼ tsp cayenne pepper
1 stalk celery, finely chopped	⅛ tsp ground cloves
Fine sea salt	1 cup/225 g black lentils
4 garlic cloves, minced	5 thin slices peeled fresh ginger
1 serrano or other small hot chile, seeded and minced	10 oz/280 g dino kale, tough stems removed, chopped
2 tsp ground cumin	¾ cup/125 g black quinoa
2 tsp ground coriander	

Heat 2 tbsp of the olive oil in a soup pot over medium-high heat. Add the onion, celery, and 1 tsp salt. Cook, stirring frequently, until the onion is soft, about 3 minutes. Add the garlic and chile and cook, stirring constantly, until very fragrant, about 1 minute. Add the cumin, coriander, cinnamon, cayenne, and cloves and cook, stirring to combine everything and to keep the spices from scorching as they sizzle and start to fill the kitchen with their aroma, about 1 minute.

Add the lentils, ginger, and 8 cups/2 L water. Bring to a boil, partially cover, and lower the heat to maintain a steady simmer. Cook until the lentils have a bit of give but aren't yet tender, about 15 minutes. Add the kale and quinoa and cook until everything is tender, about 20 minutes. Check once in a while and add more water if the soup seems too thick. When the lentils are done, season with salt (I tend to add at least another 1 or 2 tsp). Serve hot. This soup keeps very well in the fridge for 2 to 3 days and freezes nicely up to 6 months.

GREEN TEA SOUP WITH SHORT-GRAIN BROWN RICE AND TENDER GREENS

SERVES 4

This soup brings in the brown rice twice—as brown rice and as part of the tea. The particular flavor of *genmaicha*, toasted brown rice green tea, is key for this dish, so don't be tempted to use just any green tea. Pretty much everything else about this soup is remarkably open to substitution and interpretation. Try long-grain brown rice or even sweet brown rice or farro instead of short-grain brown rice, thin filets of broiled fish or leftover chicken in place of the tofu, shredded young chard leaves or watercress as stand-ins for the spinach and arugula, or blast the whole thing with hot chile oil in addition to the toasted sesame oil at the end. If you have kids around, at least let them watch as the hot tea wilts the greens in the bowl.

2 cups/380 g short-grain brown rice

1 tsp fine sea salt

12 oz/340 g soft tofu

2 green onions

8 tea bags genmaicha (toasted brown rice green tea)

4 handfuls mixed greens such as baby spinach, arugula, and/or watercress leaves

1 tsp black sesame seeds

2 tsp tamari or soy sauce

4 tsp toasted sesame oil

1 oz/30 g toasted, seasoned nori

Bring 6 cups/1.4 L water to a boil. Add the rice and salt. Lower the heat to maintain a steady simmer and cook until the rice is tender, about 45 minutes. Drain thoroughly.

Meanwhile, cut the tofu into bite-size cubes and set it aside in a warm spot to take off the chill if it was refrigerated. Cut the green onions into 2-in/5-cm lengths and then slice lengthwise into ribbons.

When the rice is just about done, bring 8 cups/2 L water to a boil in a large saucepan. Remove from the heat, add the tea bags, cover, and let steep for 5 minutes.

While the tea steeps, divide the rice between four large bowls. Add the greens and tofu to each bowl. Pour about 2 cups/480 ml of the tea over each serving. Sprinkle with the green onions and sesame seeds.

Drizzle each serving with ½ tsp tamari and 1 tsp sesame oil. Serve immediately with the toasted nori on the side for diners to crumble into their soup as they like.

BEET GREENS AND BARLEY BORSCHT

SERVES 4 TO 6

Not only is the flavor in this soup fabulous, but the soup itself is terribly satisfying to make, what with using the beets with their greens attached. Look for beets with bright, vibrant greens without too many holes or brown bits on the leaves. Hulled barley contains more fiber and nutrients than does pearled barley. It's also more difficult to find and takes longer to cook. Either is just dandy here.

½ cup/90 g hulled or pearled barley

3 beets with their greens attached

1 tbsp butter or vegetable oil

1 yellow onion, halved and thinly sliced

Fine sea salt

5 cups/1.2 L chicken, beef, or vegetable broth or water

1 tbsp fresh lemon juice, plus more if desired

Plain whole-milk yogurt or sour cream for garnish (optional)

2 tsp caraway seeds (optional)

Fresh chopped dill for garnish (optional)

Put the barley in a medium pot and add enough water to cover by about 1 in/2.5 cm. Bring to a boil, cover, and lower the heat to maintain a steady simmer. Cook until the barley is tender to the bite, about 30 minutes for pearled barley and 45 minutes for hulled. Set aside. (You can pour off any truly excess water, but there is no need to drain it—it's going into a soup, so a bit of water won't hurt anything.)

Meanwhile, preheat the oven to 350°F/180°C. Cut the beets from their greens. Scrub the beets clean, wrap them in a large sheet of foil, and place on a baking sheet. Bake until they're tender when pierced with a fork, about 45 minutes.

Let the beets sit until cool enough to handle. Peel them (their skins should slip off easily after being roasted) and grate them on the large-hole side of a box grater. Set aside. (I like the ease of peeling and grating roasted beets, but feel free to peel and grate raw beets— they will cook quickly enough in the soup.)

CONTINUED

Rinse the beet greens clean, as they often have a fair amount of grit on them. Separate the beet green stems from the beet green leaves. Chop the stems, then chop the leaves; keep the stems and leaves separate.

In a large pot over medium-high heat, melt the butter. Add the onion, beet stems, and ½ tsp salt. Cook, stirring occasionally, until the vegetables are softened, about 3 minutes. Stir in the grated beets, then add the chicken broth. Bring to a boil, lower the heat to maintain a steady simmer, and cook until the vegetables are tender, about 15 minutes.

Add the beet greens and cooked barley, and cook until the beet greens are tender and the flavors are blended, about 10 minutes.

Stir in the lemon juice. Adjust the seasoning with more salt and/or lemon juice.

Serve hot, with a dollop of yogurt and a sprinkle of caraway seeds and dill, if you like. This soup keeps nicely up to 2 days in the fridge or 6 months in the freezer.

FARRO KALE MINESTRONE

SERVES 6 TO 8

This version of minestrone has no pasta, but it does have two kinds of beans, one of which is whirled into the broth to make a thicker, richer-seeming concoction that serves quite well as a simple one-dish dinner. Whenever we finish off a hunk of Parmesan, I throw it in a plastic bag and pop it in the freezer to use the next time I make this soup. While it's not absolutely necessary, it does add a nice savory note. I prefer hearty kale here, since it can stand up to the cooking time needed to have its flavors blend in with the soup. Collard greens are, of course, a fine substitute.

2 cups/400 g dried cannellini beans or three 15-oz/430-g cans cannellini beans

1 cup/200 g dried cranberry beans or two 15-oz/430-g cans cranberry beans or chickpeas

1 cup/180 g farro

2 tbsp extra-virgin olive or vegetable oil

2 yellow onions, chopped

2 carrots, chopped

2 stalks celery, chopped

4 garlic cloves, chopped

Fine sea salt

6 cups/1.4 L chicken or vegetable broth or bean cooking liquid

1 Parmesan cheese rind (optional), plus freshly grated Parmesan cheese for serving

1 bunch kale, tough stems removed and chopped

Freshly ground pepper

Extra-virgin olive oil for drizzling

If using dried beans, rinse the cannellini and cranberry beans separately and put them in separate large bowls, add enough cool water to cover, and soak a few hours or up to overnight. (Alternatively, bring the beans, each in their own large pot and covered with water, to a boil. Cover, remove from the heat, and let sit for an hour. Proceed with these quick-soaked beans.) Drain the beans, put them each in their own large pot, and add enough water to cover by about 1 in/ 2.5 cm. Bring to a boil, lower the heat to maintain a steady simmer, and cook until the beans are tender, 20 to 60 minutes. The cooking time for beans can vary greatly, depending on how long the beans have been in storage, which is one reason why we're going to such lengths to cook them separately; the other reason is the cannellini beans get puréed and the other beans do not. If I've gone to the trouble of cooking dried beans, I reserve 6 cups/1.4 L of the bean cooking liquid to use instead of the broth for the soup before I drain the beans. Drain the beans, still keeping them separate for now.

Put the farro in a medium pot and add enough water to cover by about 1 in/2.5 cm. Bring to a boil, lower the heat to maintain a steady simmer, and cook until the farro is tender to the bite, about 30 minutes. Drain and set aside.

Heat the olive oil in a large pot over medium-high heat. Add the onions, carrots, celery, garlic, and 1 tbsp salt. Cook, stirring occasionally, until the vegetables are soft, about 5 minutes.

Add the chicken broth, cooked cannellini beans, and Parmesan rind (if using). Bring to a boil, lower the heat to maintain a steady simmer, and cook until the vegetables are very tender, about 10 minutes.

Remove the Parmesan rind and set aside. Using a blender, food processor, or immersion blender, whirl the soup until very smooth (you will need to do this in batches if you're not using an immersion blender). Return the soup and rind to the pot.

Add the cooked cranberry beans, cooked farro, and kale. Stir to combine and cook over medium-low heat until the flavors meld and the kale is tender, 10 to 15 minutes. Season with salt.

Serve hot, topped with grated Parmesan, pepper, and a drizzle of olive oil.

CHAPTER THREE

MAIN DISHES

SAVORY WHOLE-GRAIN BREAD PUDDING

SERVES 6 TO 8

While it makes a lovely supper, especially on a cold winter's night when some warming comfort may be in order, this dish is extremely well suited to brunch and shines with a piece of crisp bacon or two alongside it. I like to use a soft or sweet Gorgonzola here, pulling off bits of the pungent but soft cheese and tucking them in between the cubes of bread. That's a lot of flavor for most people, however, and a more classic take uses Gouda or Gruyère.

2 tbsp butter	½ tsp freshly ground pepper
1 loaf whole-grain bread	1 tsp fresh thyme leaves
6 eggs	10 oz/280 g kale or collard greens
2½ cups/600 ml milk	8 oz/225 g Gouda, Gruyère, blue, aged Cheddar, or other strongly flavored cheese, coarsely grated or cut into ½-in/12-mm cubes
½ cup/120 ml heavy cream	
1 tsp fine sea salt	

Preheat the oven to 350°F/180°C. Use 1 tbsp of the butter to generously grease a 2-qt/2-L baking dish.

Cut the bread into bite-size cubes, removing excess crust, if you like. If it's fresh, put it on a baking sheet and pop it in the oven for a few minutes to dry it out a bit while you prepare the other ingredients.

In a very large bowl, whisk together the eggs, milk, cream, salt, and pepper. Stir in the thyme. Add the bread cubes, stirring gently to completely coat the bread and submerge as much of it as possible in the custard mixture. Let it sit while you tend to the kale.

Cut out and discard the stems from the kale leaves and chop the leaves. Melt the remaining 1 tbsp butter in a large frying pan over high heat. Add the kale and cook, stirring frequently, until wilted and tender, about 3 minutes.

Put about half the custard-soaked bread into the prepared baking dish. Scatter the cooked kale here and there among the bread cubes. Tuck about one-third of the cheese between the pieces of kale. Top with the remaining custard-soaked bread and pour any custard left in the bowl over all of it. Arrange the remaining cheese on top. Let sit at least 30 minutes at room temperature (or up to overnight, covered, in the fridge. Bring back to cool room temperature before cooking.)

Bake until the edges are fully set and the center is just barely jiggly, about 45 minutes. Serve hot or warm. Leftovers are tasty chilled or reheated, but if you want to make it ahead of time, store covered and uncooked in the fridge, then bake right before serving.

GREENS AND GRAINS FOR BREAKFAST

I like my breakfasts savory. Leftovers from dinner are often my morning meal of choice. If you, too, like a hearty breakfast, know that these dishes are so well suited to breakfast or brunch as to warrant making them specifically for the occasion:

- Greens-Stuffed Cornmeal Cakes (page 49) served with scrambled eggs
- Green Whole-Wheat Flatbread (page 58) in lieu of toast
- Fava Greens Quiche in a Buckwheat Groat Crust (page 105) with a fruit salad or grapefruit half
- Polenta with Dandelion Relish and Soft-Boiled Eggs (page 98)
- Wild Rice Porridge with Steamed Greens (page 97)
- Savory Whole-Grain Bread Pudding (facing page) with bacon or sausage

FARRO, CHARD, AND RICOTTA CASSEROLE

SERVES 4

Most people would probably see this as a side dish, perfect to serve with broiled chops or a roasted chicken, and they would be right. I'm just as likely, though, to make this the main attraction with a salad of sliced tomatoes or thinly cut zucchini alongside. Feel free to use golden, red, or rainbow chard, but know that they will tint the entire dish!

2 cups/360 g farro

1 tsp fine sea salt

2 large bunches Swiss chard

1 tbsp extra-virgin olive oil

4 oz/115 g pancetta, chopped (optional)

4 garlic cloves, minced

1 cup/250 g ricotta cheese

¼ tsp freshly grated nutmeg

½ tsp freshly ground pepper

½ cup/60 g freshly grated Parmesan cheese

Put the farro and salt in a medium pot and add enough water to cover by about 1 in/2.5 cm. Bring to a boil, lower the heat to maintain a steady simmer, and cook until the farro is tender to the bite, about 30 minutes. Drain and set aside.

Meanwhile, cut out the thick stems from the chard leaves. Trim the stems and chop them, then chop the leaves; keep the stems and leaves separate.

Heat the olive oil in a large frying pan or sauté pan over medium-high heat. Add the pancetta and cook, stirring now and again, until it renders its fat and browns, about 5 minutes. Add the garlic and cook, stirring constantly, until fragrant, about 1 minute. Add the chard stems and 3 tbsp water. Cover and cook until the stems soften, about 3 minutes. Stir in the chard leaves (you may need to do this in batches), and cook, covered, until the leaves are wilted and tender, 3 to 4 minutes.

Preheat the broiler. Grease a 2-qt/2-L baking dish.

Put the farro in a large bowl and toss with the pancetta-chard mixture. Stir in the ricotta, and then the nutmeg and pepper. Adjust the seasoning.

Put the farro-chard mixture in the prepared baking dish. Sprinkle with the Parmesan cheese. Broil until the cheese melts and gets browned and crispy, turning the baking dish, if needed, to evenly melt and brown the cheese. Broilers vary in their power, so keep an eye on the casserole, checking every minute or so. Serve hot.

BROWN RICE BOWL

SERVES 4

The bones of this dish—hearty brown rice with stuff on top—shows up at my house a lot. Sometimes I skip the meat and hard-boiled eggs and just scramble twice as many eggs with some ginger and green onions. Or I cook some firm tofu as I do the pork. In short: Mix it up with what you have on hand. I've written the prep work into the recipe so you can see how it pulls together in the time it takes to cook the rice.

2 cups/380 g short-grain brown rice	2 tbsp tamari or soy sauce, plus more for serving
½ tsp fine sea salt	2 tbsp vegetable oil
4 eggs (optional)	2 bunches greens, such as chard, mustard greens, or kale
One 1-in/2.5-cm piece peeled fresh ginger	3 garlic cloves
1 lb/445 g ground pork	8 green onions
½ cup/120 ml sake or white wine (optional)	Fresh cilantro leaves for garnish
	Hot sauce (optional)

Bring the rice, salt, and 4 cups/960 ml water to a boil in a medium saucepan. Cover, turn the heat to low, and cook, undisturbed, for 30 minutes. Remove the lid and stir the rice to see if the rice is tender and the liquid is absorbed. If not, cover and cook 5 minutes more. Once all the liquid is absorbed, remove from the heat and let sit, covered, for 5 minutes. Fluff with a fork. Or do as I do, and set it all up in a rice cooker and forget all about it.

While the rice is cooking, cook everything else.

If using the eggs, put them in a medium saucepan and cover generously with water. Bring to a boil. Cover, remove from the heat, and let sit for 14 minutes exactly. Drain the eggs and peel under cool water. Slice and set aside.

Grate the ginger and set it aside.

Put the pork in a medium bowl and pour the sake (if using) and tamari over it. Mix gently and set aside.

Heat a large frying pan over medium-high heat. Add 1 tbsp of the vegetable oil, swirl to coat the pan, and add the pork. Cook, stirring frequently, until the pork is about halfway cooked. Some of it should have turned gray and cooked-looking, but some of it should still look raw; you don't want any of it to have started to actually brown at all. Stir in about three-quarters of the ginger and cook, stirring now and again, until the pork is cooked through and starting to brown in some spots. Transfer the pork to a bowl or plate and cover to keep warm.

Trim the greens. (If using greens with thick stems, like collards or kale, cut out and discard the stems.) Trim the stems and chop them, then chop the leaves into bite-size pieces. Mince the garlic and chop the green onions.

Return the pan to the stove over medium-high heat and add the remaining 1 tbsp vegetable oil, remaining ginger, the garlic, and green onions. Cook, stirring as the aromatics become more fragrant, about 1 minute. Add the greens, stir to combine, add 2 tbsp water, cover, and cook until the greens are tender. The timing will vary depending on the green you're using. Spinach will be done in a flash, chard or mustard greens will take 4 to 5 minutes, kale could take 10 minutes or more. Add more water to the pan to keep whatever greens you're using from sticking, if necessary.

While the greens cook, chop or mince the cilantro.

Divide the rice between four deep cereal or chili bowls. Top with the greens, pork, and a sliced hard-boiled egg, if you like. Sprinkle with cilantro and serve with tamari on the side for people to add if they like. I find those who like hot sauce tend to want to add some to this dish; serve accordingly.

RED BEANS AND COLLARD GREENS WITH BROWN RICE

SERVES 4 TO 6

Red beans and rice are a New Orleans classic. This version bucks convention not only by using brown rice but also by cooking greens along with the beans. It may not be at all traditional, but it sure saves time and dishes—plus it marries some well-matched flavors. Collards are such a classic Southern green, they make a lot of sense here, but any variety of kale can also stand up to the longer cooking time and hearty flavors of the beans.

2 cups/400 g dried red beans

2 tbsp butter, lard, or vegetable oil

1 yellow onion, diced

2 stalks celery, diced

1 green bell pepper, cored, seeded, and diced

1 carrot, diced

3 garlic cloves, minced

1 smoked ham hock or 4 oz/115 g chopped tasso or thick-cut bacon (optional)

Fine sea salt

2 bunches collard greens, trimmed and chopped

2 cups/380 g long-grain brown rice

Tabasco or other hot sauce for serving

Rinse the beans, put them in a large bowl, add enough cool water to cover, and soak for a few hours or up to overnight. (Alternatively, bring the beans, covered with water, to a boil. Cover, remove from the heat, and let sit for 1 hour. Proceed with these quick-soaked beans.)

Melt the butter in a large pot over medium-high heat. Add the onion, celery, bell pepper, and carrot and cook, stirring a bit, until the vegetables are softened, about 3 minutes. Add the garlic and cook, stirring again, until fragrant, about 1 minute.

Drain the beans and add them to the pot with the ham hock (if using). Add enough water to cover everything. Bring to a boil, lower the heat to maintain a steady simmer, and cook, stirring now and again, until it smells of cooked beans and the beans are starting to be tender but are still a bit raw in the center. Add 2 tsp salt (or more, you will likely need quite a bit—there is a lot of water in that pot!) and the collard greens. Continue simmering until the beans and collards are tender. The timing on this varies tremendously—older dried beans may take well over 1½ hours whereas fresher dried beans may be done in 45 minutes.

Bring the rice, 1 tsp salt, and 4½ cups/1 L water to a boil in a medium saucepan. Cover, turn the heat to low, and cook, undisturbed, for 45 minutes. Remove the lid and stir the rice to see if the rice is tender and the liquid is absorbed. If not, cover and cook 5 minutes more. Once all the liquid is absorbed, take the pot off the heat and let sit, covered, for 5 minutes. Fluff with a fork. If there is a rice cooker in the kitchen, throw everything in there instead.

When the beans, collards, and rice are done, shred any meat off the ham hock and discard the bone. Add the meat to the beans. Adjust the seasoning.

Serve the rice topped with the beans. Make sure to have hot sauce on the table for those who like it.

PEA GREENS AND TOFU OVER SESAME BROWN RICE

SERVES 4

Pea greens are the tender shoots and tendrils of pea plants. You'll find them in giant tangled heaps at some farm stands and markets in spring and early summer. This quick, fresh stir-fry is a great way to use any tender green—spinach, for example, is a fine substitute. Chopped mustard greens are also tasty here. Silken firm tofu, also called Japanese-style tofu and often sold in shelf-stable aseptic packages, has a much smoother texture than regular tofu that is particularly pleasing here; any firm tofu will work, though.

1 cup/190 g long-grain brown rice

½ tsp fine sea salt

2 tbsp mixed black and white sesame seeds

1 tbsp vegetable, canola, or grapeseed oil

1 spring onion, trimmed and finely chopped

3 garlic cloves, minced

1 tbsp finely grated peeled fresh ginger

¼ cup/60 ml rice wine, sake, dry white wine, or chicken or vegetable broth

2 tsp tamari or soy sauce

8 oz/225 g pea greens

12 oz/340 g silken firm tofu, cut into bite-size pieces

¼ cup/10 g minced fresh cilantro leaves (optional)

Bring the rice, salt, and 2¼ cups/540 ml water to a boil in a medium saucepan. Cover, turn the heat to low, and cook, undisturbed, for 45 minutes. Remove the lid and stir the rice to see if the rice is tender and the liquid is absorbed. If not, cover and cook for 5 minutes more. Once all the liquid is absorbed, take the pot off the heat and let sit, covered, for 5 minutes. Fluff with a fork. Of course, if I had a rice cooker on hand, I'd use it.

Meanwhile, heat a small frying pan over medium-high heat. Add the sesame seeds and cook, swirling the pan or stirring frequently, until the seeds are toasted, 3 to 5 minutes. Set aside to cool.

While the rice rests, heat a wok or large sauté pan over high heat. Add the vegetable oil, swirl to coat the pan, and add the spring onion. Cook, stirring constantly, until the spring onion is soft, about 2 minutes. Add the garlic and ginger, and stir as everything comes to a sizzle. Pour in the rice wine and tamari, and cook, stirring as the liquid evaporates, about 1 minute.

CONTINUED

Add the pea greens, cover, and cook until wilted and just barely tender, about 3 minutes. Gently stir in the tofu, cover, and cook until heated through, about 1 minute.

Stir the toasted sesame seeds into the cooked rice. Serve the pea greens and tofu over the rice, and garnish with the cilantro, if you like.

WILD RICE PORRIDGE WITH STEAMED GREENS

SERVES 4

My family eats versions of this with shocking frequency at home, especially in the winter. Since the garnishes are usually based on what I can scrounge out of the fridge, it's never quite the same. And since everyone gets to top their own bowl, the versions on the table together aren't even the same. I'm a home-chicken-broth maker and user; if you're using store-bought broth, go ahead and use 4 cups/960 ml broth and 2 cups/480 ml water to keep the final porridge from being too salty or having that concentrated-broth flavor.

1 cup/160 g wild rice

1 cup/190 g short-, medium-, or long-grain brown rice

6 cups/1.4 L chicken or vegetable broth

2 tbsp rice wine or sake (optional)

1 tbsp grated peeled fresh ginger

1 bunch greens, such as spinach, chard, kale, or collard greens, stems removed, if tough, and chopped or cut into ribbons

Garnishes (list follows)

Put the wild rice, brown rice, chicken broth, rice wine, and ginger in a large pot. Bring to a boil, partially cover, and lower the heat to maintain a steady simmer. Cook, stirring occasionally, until porridge-like, about 50 minutes.

Put the greens in a steamer basket and set over boiling water, covered, until wilted and tender, about 3 minutes for spinach, 5 minutes for chard, and up to 10 minutes for kale or collard greens.

Divide the porridge between four bowls and top each with a portion of the steamed greens to serve. Allow diners to add whatever they like from the following list to garnish.

GARNISHES

- Coarsely grated or diced baked tofu
- Shredded cooked chicken or duck
- Shredded or diced cooked pork
- Minced green onion, chives, or garlic chives
- Minced fresh cilantro
- Minced lemongrass (tender inner core only)
- Finely shredded carrot
- Finely shredded or diced zucchini
- Shredded daikon radish
- Sliced fish cake
- Toasted and crumbled seaweed
- Sesame seeds
- Toasted sesame oil
- Hot chile oil
- Soy sauce or tamari

POLENTA WITH DANDELION RELISH AND SOFT-BOILED EGGS

SERVES 4

The interesting thing here is the dandelion relish. Inspired by the currant-and-pine-nut-laden chard tarts of Italy, the relish adds a flavorful kick to homey polenta and eggs. Or use it as a spread in sandwiches. Know that despite what may be good instincts in other situations, olive oil brings too strong a flavor to this relish. While the delicate garlic flavor of green garlic (immature garlic pulled to thin the garden rows) and garlic scapes (the curled flower stalks of hardneck garlic) is lovely here, if those are out of season or not available where you are, green onions are perfect as well. For a softer, creamier polenta, try using ricotta instead of the Parmesan.

4¼ cups/1.1 L chicken or vegetable broth or water	1 green garlic, garlic scape, or green onion, chopped
1 cup/150 g polenta	1 tbsp pistachio, pine nut, hemp, or vegetable oil
¾ tsp fine sea salt	1 tsp agave syrup or sugar
2 tbsp freshly grated Parmesan cheese (optional)	2 tbsp pine nuts
2 tbsp butter	2 tbsp dried currants or blueberries
4 oz/115 g dandelion greens, stems removed and leaves chopped	4 eggs

Bring the broth to a boil in a medium saucepan. With the broth boiling, sprinkle in the polenta while stirring the liquid. Stir in ½ tsp of the salt and keep stirring until the entire mixture boils again. Lower the heat to maintain a steady simmer and cover. Stir the polenta every few minutes until it is thick and tender, about 25 minutes. (Traditionally polenta is stirred constantly while cooking—go ahead and do this if you like, but it's not absolutely necessary. Polenta experts can, I am sure, tell the difference; most of us, however, are not polenta aficionados and will find ourselves quite happy with the less-stirred version, particularly if we use that time to make a yummy dandelion relish.) Stir the Parmesan into the polenta, if you like. Adjust the seasoning, and stir in the butter. Remove from the heat and cover.

CONTINUED

Meanwhile, bring a medium pot of water to a boil.

In a blender or food processor, pulse the dandelion greens, green garlic, pistachio oil, agave syrup, and remaining ¼ tsp salt to form a rough purée. Add the pine nuts and currants and pulse to combine and make everything into a chunky relish.

When the water boils, gently submerge the eggs and cook for 3 minutes for a completely runny yolk and some not-quite-set whites, 4 minutes for a yolk with barely set edges (my favorite), 5 minutes for a yolk that is starting to firm up on the edges but is still a bit runny in the center, and 6 minutes for a yolk that is starting to set throughout. Drain and peel the eggs under cool water.

Divide the polenta among four wide bowls, and top with a peeled soft-boiled egg and a spoonful of dandelion relish.

Extra dandelion relish keeps for up to 1 week in the fridge.

BARLEY "RISOTTO" WITH KALE AND MUSHROOMS

SERVES 4

As much as I love the extra fiber and minimal processing of hulled barley, it won't get that creamy-starchy texture that allows one to even think about calling this "risotto," so I call for pearled barley here. Why not use short-grain brown rice, you ask? It just doesn't take to this cooking method and leaves one wishing for Arborio rice. The barley manages to be at once its own thing but also magically fits the "risotto" mold.

2 tbsp butter

1 small yellow onion, finely chopped

½ tsp fine sea salt

8 oz/225 g mushrooms, stems finely chopped and caps sliced

10 oz/280 g kale, stems discarded, finely chopped

2 cups/360 g pearled barley

1 cup/240 ml dry white wine

6 cups/1.4 L chicken, vegetable, or mushroom broth

Freshly grated Parmesan cheese for garnish

Melt the butter in a large saucepan or small pot over medium-high heat. Add the onion and salt. Cook, stirring frequently, until the onion is soft, about 3 minutes. Turn the heat to high and add the mushrooms. Cook, stirring frequently, until the mushrooms release their liquid, about 5 minutes. Add the kale and cook, stirring frequently, until wilted, about 2 minutes.

Rinse the barley, shake off as much water as possible, add it to the pan, and stir to combine everything. Pour in the wine and cook, stirring constantly, until the liquid is absorbed, about 5 minutes.

Add the chicken broth and stir to combine. Bring to a boil, partially cover, and lower the heat to maintain a steady simmer. Cook, stirring every few minutes, until the liquid is absorbed and the barley is tender, about 30 minutes.

Serve hot, garnished with Parmesan.

BUTTERED BUCKWHEAT WITH FENUGREEK KALE AND SPICY YELLOW SPLIT PEAS

SERVES 6

Yes, this does seem like a lot of paprika. Don't worry about that; the heat comes from the dried chile in the spiced butter. Feel free to use less of that, if you'd like. And yes, the spiced butter uses lots of different spices. While the spices do work together in a balanced and delicious way, you can feel free to use whatever combination you can cobble together. The key is the paprika; whatever else you can or can't add to the mix, the spiced butter will still add plenty of pizzazz.

SPLIT PEAS

1 cup/200 g yellow split peas or chana dal (hulled and split chickpeas)

5 thin slices peeled fresh ginger

1 tsp turmeric

1 tsp fine sea salt

KALE

20 oz/560 g kale

1 tbsp butter

¼ tsp ground fenugreek

1 yellow onion, minced

4 garlic cloves, minced

2 serranos or other small hot chiles, seeded and minced

1 tbsp grated fresh ginger

½ tsp fine sea salt

Champagne vinegar for sprinkling (optional)

BUCKWHEAT

2 cups/340 g toasted buckwheat groats

½ tsp fine sea salt

SPICED BUTTER

4 tbsp butter

1 tbsp hot paprika

1 tsp crumbled dried red chile or red chile flakes

½ tsp ground cumin

¼ tsp ground cardamom

¼ tsp ground coriander

¼ tsp fenugreek seeds or ground fenugreek

¼ tsp freshly ground pepper

¼ tsp ground ginger

¼ tsp turmeric

⅛ tsp ground allspice or ground cloves

⅛ tsp ground cinnamon

TO MAKE THE SPLIT PEAS: Rinse the split peas and put them in a medium pot with 4 cups/960 ml water, the ginger, and turmeric. Bring to a boil, skim the surface of any foam, and simmer, partially covered, until the split peas are tender, about 30 minutes. Add more water, if needed, to keep from getting too thick or sticking to the bottom of the pot. Stir in the salt. Set aside.

TO MAKE THE KALE: Trim off and discard the tough ends of the kale stems, chop the remaining stems and leaves all together; bite-size pieces are good, thin ribbons are even better. Melt the butter in a large sauté pan or wide, shallow pot over high heat. Add the fenugreek and cook, stirring as it sizzles, about 30 seconds. Add the onion, garlic, chiles, ginger, and salt. Cook, stirring frequently as the aromatics soften, about 2 minutes. Stir in the kale. Add ½ cup/120 ml water, cover, and turn the heat to medium-low. Cook, stirring now and again, until the kale is very tender, about 40 minutes. Remove the cover and continue cooking to let any excess water evaporate, about 5 minutes. Lightly sprinkle the kale with vinegar, if you like. Set aside.

TO MAKE THE BUCKWHEAT: Bring 4 cups/960 ml water to a boil in a large saucepan. Add the buckwheat groats and salt. Cover, turn heat to low, and cook, maintaining a steady simmer, undisturbed, for 15 minutes. Remove from the heat and let sit for 5 minutes. Uncover and fluff with a fork. If the directions on the package for the buckwheat groats you have are much different from the ones here, follow the package directions; different varieties of buckwheat can cook up quite differently. Set aside.

TO MAKE THE SPICED BUTTER: When everything else is ready to serve, melt the butter in a saucepan over medium heat. Add all the spices at once and cook, stirring until fragrant, about 30 seconds. Remove from the heat.

Spoon the split peas, kale, and buckwheat alongside one another into six shallow pasta bowls. Drizzle the spiced butter over the split peas before serving. If some butter spills over to the kale and buckwheat, so be it.

FAVA GREENS QUICHE IN A BUCKWHEAT GROAT CRUST

SERVES 4 TO 6

This is so cool. Toasted buckwheat groats coat the pie pan and cool into a crust along with the filling. That's right, no pastry to make or roll out. If you have access to fava greens (usually from a garden or at a farm stand), their slightly nutty flavor is lovely with the eggs in the quiche, but spinach, or really any green as long as it's cooked until tender, is a fine substitute for hard-to-find fava greens. I found the delicate greens and silky custard of the quiche lost a bit of their charm and were even overpowered when I used cheese, but die-hard cheese lovers can sprinkle on all the grated Gruyère or Gouda they like.

¾ cup/120 g toasted buckwheat groats

1 tbsp butter

2 shallots, minced

4 oz/115 g fava greens

1½ tsp fine sea salt

3 eggs

1 cup/240 ml milk

½ cup/120 ml heavy cream

Preheat the oven to 350°F/180°C.

Grease a 9-in/23-cm pie pan. Pour in the buckwheat groats, patting them against the prepared pan evenly, along the bottom and up the sides.

Melt the butter in a large sauté or frying pan over medium-high heat. Add the shallots and cook, stirring frequently, until soft, about 3 minutes. Add the fava greens and ½ tsp of the salt and cook, stirring often, until the greens are wilted and tender, about 5 minutes.

In a large bowl, whisk together the eggs, milk, cream, and remaining 1 tsp salt.

Gently arrange the fava greens over the buckwheat groats and carefully pour in the custard. Bake until the edges are fully set and the center is just barely jiggly, about 40 minutes. Let cool to room temperature before slicing. This is best eaten the day it is made but will keep, covered and chilled, overnight. Don't try to reheat it; the eggs will get rubbery.

BUCKWHEAT GALETTES STUFFED WITH WALNUTS AND BLUE CHEESE TOPPED WITH ARUGULA SALAD

MAKES 12 GALETTES

My absolute favorite classic crêpe is not ham and cheese nor, to my son's dismay, is it made with Nutella. It's walnut and blue cheese served with a simple salad on top. Sounds crazy, but it's crazy delicious. I've put a spin on that here by using flavorful arugula for the salad. Also, while Roquefort is the classic choice, I prefer soft Gorgonzola in these galettes (what savory crêpes made with buckwheat flour are usually called). If you've never made crêpes, know that the first one most likely won't turn out. Worry not. There is enough batter for 13 or 14, so you can mess a few up. For thin crêpes with lacy browning, be sure to let the batter rest—this allows the flour to fully absorb the moisture and for any air bubbles to get out of the way. To speed the process of getting a silky smooth batter, I try to start off with flat beer, but if you've just opened the bottle, that's okay—just avoid adding any actual foam.

2 cups/480 ml milk

8 tbsp/115 g butter

1 tsp fine sea salt

1 tsp sugar

1 cup/240 ml flat beer

4 eggs

¾ cup/120 g buckwheat flour

1½ cups/180 g whole-wheat pastry flour

3 tbsp grapeseed, canola, or other neutral-flavored salad oil

1 tsp Champagne vinegar

½ tsp dry ground mustard

¼ tsp freshly ground pepper

6 handfuls arugula leaves

1 cup/100 g walnuts

12 oz/340 g blue cheese

In a small saucepan, warm the milk, 6 tbsp/85 g of the butter, ½ tsp of the salt, and the sugar over medium heat until the butter melts. Let cool slightly.

Pour the milk-butter mixture and the beer into a blender and whirl to combine. Add the eggs and whirl to combine. Add the buckwheat flour and pastry flour and whirl, again, to combine. Cover and chill for at least 2 hours, or up to 2 days.

In a large bowl, whisk together the grapeseed oil, vinegar, ground mustard, pepper, and remaining ½ tsp salt. Put the arugula on top and set aside (don't toss yet!).

CONTINUED

In a large frying pan over medium-high heat, toast the walnuts. Cook, stirring frequently, until the walnuts start turning a bit darker and smelling a bit more walnutty. Watch them carefully—nuts go from toasted to burnt in the blink of an eye! Take them off the heat and transfer to a plate. They will continue toasting a bit as they sit. When the walnuts are cool, chop coarsely.

Heat a 10-in/25-cm frying pan over high heat. (If you have a nonstick pan, you may want to use it, but I find using a hot pan and brushing it liberally with melted butter works well as long as I'm willing to sacrifice the first crêpe or two to the process; those first specimens seem to "cure" the pan, or maybe they just allow the cook some time to get the heat just right and master the method.)

Once the pan is hot, lower the heat to medium and add about ½ tsp butter, allowing it to melt. Ladle in about ¼ cup/60 ml of the batter, swirling the pan as you do so to completely coat the bottom. Cook, undisturbed, until bubbles form on top of the galette and the bottom is browned, about 1 minute. Use a thin spatula or table knife to make sure the edges aren't sticking to the pan, then flip the galette. Shake the pan vigorously to make sure the galette doesn't stick. Cook until browned on the second side, 1 minute more. Transfer the galette to a plate and repeat with the remaining butter and batter. You won't need to add quite as much butter as you make more, as the pan sort of cures as you go. If the galettes are taking much longer or shorter to cook and brown, adjust the heat. You can layer parchment or waxed paper between the cooked galettes as you stack them, but I find they stack and come apart quite nicely if kept at room temperature. (If you want to freeze them, however, be sure to use paper to separate them.)

To fill the galettes, you have two options: To fill them as you cook them, spread 1 oz/30 g of the cheese and just over 1 tbsp of the walnuts on half the galette after you flip it. Once it's cooked through, fold the galette over the filling. Or, what I prefer, is to fill the galettes after they've all been cooked. Put each galette back in a medium-hot pan, arrange a portion of cheese and walnuts on half of it and, once it's heated through, fold the galette over to encase the filling. The advantage of the second method is twofold: You can make all the galettes ahead of time and you can use a large griddle or have more than one pan going to reheat and fill more than one galette at once.

Just before serving, toss the arugula with the dressing at the bottom of the bowl to coat. Put a portion of dressed arugula on top of or alongside each galette. Serve while the galettes are hot.

SWISS CHARD LITTLE DOVES WITH TOMATO SAUCE

SERVES 4 TO 6

Tender but flavorful Swiss chard leaves wrap up a savory filling of whole grains and chopped chard stems before being baked in a simple tomato sauce in this modern take on *golubtsy* ("little doves"), or stuffed cabbage. I like to buy extra chard to guarantee plenty of leaves large enough and intact enough to make single bundles out of them, but feel free to cobble two leaves together for some of the packets. Red chard or rainbow chard also work nicely in this recipe; since everything is cooked in a tomato sauce, the slight "bleeding" from the red stalks will be well hidden.

½ cup/90 g pearled barley	½ tsp red chile flakes (optional)
½ cup/85 g quinoa	1 yellow onion
One 28-oz/800-g can whole peeled tomatoes, drained	12 large Swiss chard leaves
2 roasted red bell peppers, peeled	¼ cup/30 g chopped toasted walnuts
4 tbsp butter	1 tbsp extra-virgin olive oil
½ tsp fine sea salt, plus 1 tbsp	½ tsp freshly ground pepper

Bring a large pot of water to a boil.

Rinse the barley and quinoa and drain. Put the barley and quinoa in a large bowl and cover with cool water.

Whirl the tomatoes and roasted red peppers in a blender or food processor until smooth. In a wide sauté pan over medium-high heat, combine the puréed tomato mixture, butter, ½ tsp salt, and chile flakes (if using). Cut the stem end off the onion and trim the root end, leaving the core at the root to hold the onion together. Cut the onion in half through the root end, peel the halves, and add them to the tomato mixture.

Bring the tomato mixture just to a boil, stirring in the butter as it melts, then lower the heat to maintain a gentle simmer. Cook, undisturbed, until the butter separates out from the tomatoes and floats on the top, about 30 minutes. Adjust the seasoning.

While the sauce simmers, rinse the chard leaves and cut out the stems. Finely chop the stems and put them in a large bowl.

CONTINUED

Add the 1 tbsp salt to the now-boiling water. Blanch the chard leaves by dipping them into the boiling water until they wilt, about 30 seconds. Drain the leaves and rinse them thoroughly with cold water to cool them quickly (this will also set the green color). Gently squeeze as much water out of them as you can, open them up again, and set aside.

Drain the barley and quinoa and add to the chard stems along with the walnuts. Drizzle with the olive oil and sprinkle in the black pepper. Toss to combine.

Working with one leaf at a time, lay it on a work surface, put 3 or 4 tbsp filling at one end of the leaf, bring the shorter end of the leaf up and over the filling, fold in the sides to encase the filling, and then roll it up to the longer end so the filling is completely encased and the whole thing makes a plump rectangular bundle. Or place the filling in the center of a leaf and simply fold all the sides over the filling and tuck in any corners that stick out. The chard leaves are flexible, so you, too, have some flexibility when shaping them. Both the barley and the quinoa will expand as they cook, so no matter which method you use, be sure to wrap the leaves loosely around the filling. Repeat with the remaining chard leaves and filling. You should have about twelve stuffed chard leaves.

Remove the onion halves from the tomato sauce when it's done simmering. Stir in 1 cup/240 ml water and bring the sauce back to a simmer. Set the filled chard leaves directly in the tomato sauce in the pan in a single layer—the sauce will come about one-third to one-half of the way up their sides. Cover and simmer until the barley and quinoa are tender, about 40 minutes. Check on the pan after about 20 minutes and then every 5 minutes or so. If the tomato sauce starts to stick to the bottom of the pan, add 1 tbsp water along the edges of the pan and adjust the heat to keep a steady and gentle simmer going until 40 minutes have passed and the filling is cooked through and tender.

Serve the stuffed chard leaves hot with a bit of extra sauce under, over, or alongside them, as you like. These keep nicely, covered and chilled, for up to 2 days. Reheat gently, covered and over low heat, on the stove, or cover with foil and reheat in a 350°F/180°C oven.

BRAISED CHICKEN WITH FARRO, KALE, AND WINTER SQUASH

SERVES 4 TO 6

This dinner is the culinary equivalent of a giant cashmere blanket. Cozy and comforting, and so easy you don't really need to think about it, yet oddly rich and fabulous. One pot equals a complete dinner, although a crispy tossed green salad with a sharp, acidic dressing on the side wouldn't be out of order.

1 tsp vegetable oil

8 bone-in, skin-on chicken thighs

2 shallots, thinly sliced

1 tsp fine sea salt

¼ cup/60 ml dry sherry

1 lb/455 g winter squash, such as acorn, butternut, or kabocha, peeled, seeded, and cut into bite-size pieces

10 oz/280 g dino kale, stems discarded, chopped

1 cup/180 g farro or spelt

1 cup/240 ml chicken broth

Handful of pomegranate seeds (optional)

Start off with a pan or pot at least 12 in/30.5 cm across. The heavier the better; cast iron is ideal. Heat it over medium-high heat, add the vegetable oil, and swirl to coat the bottom of the pan. Set the chicken, skin-side down, in the pan and cook, undisturbed, until the skin has rendered off much of its fat and become beautifully, deeply browned, 4 to 5 minutes. Transfer the chicken to a plate or platter.

Do not clean the pan; just pour out any excess fat, leaving a thin coat in the pan, and return it to the stove. Add the shallots and salt, and cook, stirring frequently, until softened, about 2 minutes.

Add the sherry and cook, stirring and scraping up the browned bits from the chicken, until the sherry is pretty much evaporated.

Add the squash and stir so it's coated. Stir in the kale and cook, stirring frequently, until wilted and just a bit tender, about 3 minutes. Add the farro and stir to combine.

Add the chicken broth, bring to a simmer, and set the chicken pieces, skin-side up, on top of the farro and vegetables. Cover and simmer until the farro and vegetables are tender, the liquid is absorbed, and the chicken is cooked through, about 30 minutes.

Preheat the broiler, uncover the pan, and set it under the broiler to crisp up the chicken skin, rotating the pan as necessary.

Serve all together. Garnish with pomegranate seeds, if you like.

CLAMS AND MUSSELS IN SPICY TOMATOES OVER QUINOA

SERVES 4

Not only does the quinoa soak up the spicy broth in this dish beautifully, but the whole dinner can be pulled together in the 25 minutes it takes to cook the quinoa from start to finish. I like the mix of clams and mussels, but one or the other is plenty tasty. I tend to use canned tomatoes to keep this dish speedy, but there's no reason not to peel, seed, and chop fresh tomatoes instead.

1 cup/170 g quinoa

1¼ tsp fine sea salt

2 tbsp extra-virgin olive oil

4 garlic cloves, thinly sliced

3 whole dried red chiles or ½ tsp red chile flakes

8 green onions, chopped

8 canned peeled, seeded tomatoes, chopped

1 cup/240 ml dry white wine

4 lb/1.8 kg clams and/or mussels, scrubbed clean and debearded

4 handfuls arugula leaves

Heat a medium saucepan over high heat. Add the quinoa and lower the heat to medium-high. Cook, stirring continuously, until the quinoa is nicely toasted, about 3 minutes. Add 1 cup/240 ml water and ¾ tsp of the salt and bring to a boil. Cover, turn the heat to low, and cook, undisturbed, for 15 minutes. Remove from the heat, leaving the pot covered, and let sit for 5 minutes. Fluff with a fork.

Meanwhile, heat a large pot over medium-high heat. Add the olive oil, swirl to coat the pot, and add the garlic. Cook, stirring, until the garlic is fragrant, about 30 seconds. Add the dried chiles and cook, still stirring, until the garlic just turns golden. Add the green onions and remaining ½ tsp salt. Cook, all the time stirring, until the green onions are soft, about 1 minute. Add the tomatoes and stir to combine, smashing them a bit as you do so. Add the wine, bring to a boil, and cook until the liquid in the pot is reduced by about half, 10 to 15 minutes.

Add the clams and mussels to the pot and layer the arugula on top. Cover and cook until all the shellfish open, 5 to 10 minutes. Discard any shellfish that don't open.

Stir to coat the shellfish and arugula with the yummy tomato mixture on the bottom of the pot.

Divide the quinoa among four shallow bowls. Top with the shellfish and even amounts of the sauce.

Serve immediately. Like most shellfish dishes, this one doesn't store well.

GREENS-WRAPPED FISH WITH LEMON-DILL CRACKED WHEAT

SERVES 4

Chard, collard greens, kale, mustard greens, turnip greens—any hefty cooking green works to wrap flavorful fish to give them just a wee bit of protection against the heat of the flame. You can, of course, gut and clean the fish yourself, but I always ask my fishmonger to do it for me; I can do it if I have to, but experience has taught me that I'm a wimp and the viscera makes me queasy. If you want to use quicker-cooking bulgur instead of cracked wheat, just put the same amount of bulgur in a bowl and pour half the amount of broth over it, cover, and let sit until the bulgur is tender and has absorbed the broth, about 15 minutes.

8 large leaves kale or other hearty cooking greens

8 fresh sardines or small trout, gutted and cleaned

¼ cup/10 g minced fresh chives

Fine sea salt

Freshly ground pepper

Vegetable oil for brushing

3 cups/720 ml chicken or vegetable broth

1½ cups/225 g cracked wheat

1 tbsp melted butter or extra-virgin olive oil

1 tbsp lemon juice

½ cup/20 g chopped fresh dill

Bring a large pot or large frying pan of water to a boil. Cut out and discard the thick stem from each kale leaf. Dip the leaves into the boiling water to blanch them, about 1 minute. Drain and rinse with cold water until the leaves have cooled off.

Set each sardine on a leaf. Sprinkle the inside of the sardine with chives and season with salt and pepper. Wrap each fish in the leaf—I find just rolling it up works well. Set the fish on a baking sheet. Brush the bundles with vegetable oil.

Bring the chicken broth to a boil in a medium saucepan. Add the cracked wheat and give it a stir, letting everything come back to a boil. Cover, remove from the heat, and let sit for 15 minutes; the wheat should be tender and the broth absorbed. If there's still liquid at the bottom of the pot, return to the heat and cook, stirring fairly frequently, until the broth is cooked off.

Meanwhile, heat the grill to medium-high heat; you should be able to hold your hand about 1 in/2.5 cm above the cooking grate for 3 to 4 seconds. Set the wrapped fish bundles on the grill, cook for 5 minutes, turn the bundles, and cook until the fish is hot and flaky all the way through and the green is tender and browned on both sides, 5 minutes more.

Toss the cracked wheat with the butter and lemon juice. Season with salt and pepper and stir in the dill. Serve hot with the greens-wrapped sardines on top or on the side.

QUINOA-CRUSTED TILAPIA ON WILTED RAINBOW CHARD

SERVES 4

The quinoa coating on the fish in this recipe will make you wonder why on Earth anyone ever used bread crumbs. Crunchy, nutty, crisp, and yummy—it's really everything you want in a fish coating.

1 cup/170 g quinoa	**1 shallot, minced**
¾ tsp fine sea salt	**1 bunch rainbow chard, stems and leaves separated and chopped**
1 egg	
Four 4-oz/115-g tilapia fillets	**1 tbsp vegetable oil**
3 tbsp butter	**2 lemons, cut into wedges**
	Freshly ground pepper

Put the quinoa in a fine-mesh strainer and rinse several times with cool water. Put the rinsed quinoa, 1 cup/240 ml water, and ½ tsp of the salt in a small saucepan. Bring to a boil, cover, and lower the heat to maintain a gentle simmer. Cook, undisturbed, until the quinoa is tender and the water is absorbed, about 15 minutes. Spread the cooked quinoa on a baking sheet and let it cool and dry off, at least 1 hour at room temperature or covered and chilled overnight.

Beat the egg with 2 tbsp water in a shallow bowl. Set yourself up for success by setting it on the left and the tray of quinoa on the right directly in front of you on a counter or other work surface (egg on right and quinoa on left if you're left-handed).

Pat the tilapia fillets dry. Working with one at a time, dip it into the egg, turning to coat it completely and letting any excess egg drip off and back into the bowl before laying the fillet in the quinoa and heavily coating it. I assure you things will go more smoothly and quickly—and there will be much less hand washing between fillets—if you make an effort to use your left hand to deal with the uncoated fish and the egg-coated fillet and your right hand to deal with the quinoa and the quinoa-coated fillet. Set the coated fillet on a large plate or platter. Repeat with the remaining fillets, keeping one hand wet with fish and egg and the other hand somewhat dry with cooked quinoa and coated fish.

Melt 1 tbsp of the butter in a large frying pan or sauté pan over medium-high heat. Add the shallot, chard stems, and remaining ¼ tsp salt and cook, stirring frequently, until the stems soften, about 3 minutes. Add the chard leaves and cook, stirring occasionally, until wilted and tender, about 5 minutes.

Meanwhile, melt the remaining 2 tbsp butter in a second large frying pan over medium-high heat. When the butter stops foaming, add the oil. Carefully lay the fillets in the pan and cook, undisturbed, until the quinoa crisps and browns, 4 to 5 minutes. Gently flip the fillets and cook until the fish is cooked through and the second side is nicely browned, 4 to 5 minutes more. If you don't have a pan large enough to hold four fillets, use two pans or cook them in batches, keeping the first batch warm in a 250°F/120°C oven while the second batch cooks.

Spritz the chard with some juice from a couple of the lemon wedges and divide it evenly between four plates. Lay a fillet either alongside or on top of the greens. Serve with more lemon wedges and freshly ground pepper for diners to add themselves.

INDEX